ALONE ACROSS THE ARCTIC

One Woman's Epic Journey

by Dog Team

To Eric Shirley
Happy Trails!
Pam Flowers

Pam Flowers

with Ann Dixon

Alaska Northwest Books®

Anchorage • Portland

To my friend Dorothy Nicholson, who never once stopped believing in me, and whom I'll never forget. — P. F.

To Nanette, Marcia, Kaylene, Monica, and Michelle, who encourage me on the writing journey. — A. D.

▲ *Robert*

Text © 2001 by Pam Flowers and Ann Dixon
All photographs except for the one on page 32 © 2001 by Pam Flowers
Illustration © 2001 by David Totten
Photograph on page 32 is from the book *Across Arctic America* by
Knud Rasmussen, published in 1927 by G.P. Putnam's Sons.

Library of Congress Cataloging-in-Publication Data
Flowers, Pam.
    Alone across the Arctic : one woman's epic journey by dog team / Pam Flowers with
Ann Dixon.
        p. cm
Includes index.
    ISBN 0-88240-547-0 (hardbound) — ISBN 0-88240-539- X (softbound)
1. Flowers, Pam — Journeys — Arctic regions. 2. Flowers, Pam — Journeys — Alaska.
3. Flowers, Pam — Journeys — Canada, Northern. 4. Arctic regions — Description and
travel. 5. Alaska — Description and travel. 6. Canada, Northern — Description and
travel. 7. Dogsledding — Arctic regions. 8. Dogsledding — Alaska. 9. Dogsledding —
Canada, Northern. I. Dixon, Ann. II. Title.
G635. F56 A3 2001
919.804 — dc21   2001000636

Fourth Printing 2005

Alaska Northwest Books®
An imprint of Graphic Arts Center Publishing Company
P.O. Box 10306
Portland, Oregon 97296-0306
503-226-2402; www.gacpc.com

President: Charles M. Hopkins
Associate Publisher: Douglas A. Pfeiffer
Editorial Staff: Timothy W. Frew, Ellen Harkins Wheat, Tricia Brown,
    Kathy Matthews, Jean Andrews, Jean Bond-Slaughter
Copy Editor: Linda Gunnarson
Production Staff: Richard L. Owsiany, Susan Dupere
Design: Constance Bollen, cb graphics
Map: Gray Mouse Graphics

Printed in the United States of America

Acknowledgments

I would like to thank the following people for all the welcome help each of you gave. Some of you believed in me and encouraged me along the way. Many of you met me as a stranger in your town and gave me good food, a warm place to sleep, and a badly needed shower. Others helped place caches, find Douggie, or gave directions and useful advice. Some of you read the manuscript and made many helpful suggestions so we could tell this story.

I've made a sincere and thoughtful effort to include everyone in these acknowledgments. If anyone has been left off this list, it is by accident, and I apologize for the error.

Dorothy Nicholson; Natalie and Earl Norris; Alice Holinger, Bridgette Preston, Jeff Veteto, Larry Eichmann, Paul Maloney, Bill Kuper, Mike Bowman, Doyle Deason, Craig George, Geoff Carroll, Adam Linn, Doug Barrette, Doreen Church; Eddie and Millie Gruben; Mary Lane, Peter Green, Andy Kudluk; Michelle and Alex Buchan; John Nantoak, Bill Lyall; Steve and Brenda Mercer; Alfred Rowan, Jill, and Mark Taylor; Rawley Garrels, Peter Semotiuk, David Amagana; Henry, Lena, and Karen; Salomie, Gideon, Sean, Aida, and Naomi Qitsualik; Naavee, Mark, and Jason Tootiak; Charlie and Carey Cahill; Martha Dwyer; Maurice, Patsy, and Tara Randall; Lori and Doug Nichols; Brian Ladoon, Judy Langford, John Norris; the people at Calm Air; the people at VIA Rail; the people at U-Haul; Marie Barnes, Jean Holinger, Sallie Greenwood, Matt Maniaci, Diana Conway, Kathy Pruzan, and Nori Dixon; and Ellen Wheat, Tricia Brown, Kathy Matthews, Susan Dupere, Linda Gunnarson, Constance Bollen, and Dave Totten.

A special thank-you to Knud Rasmussen, Anarulunguaq, and Miteq for inspiring me. We all need heroes.

Most of all I thank my eight best friends: Douggie-Dog, Anna, Mighty Matt, Alice, Lucy, Robert, Sojo, and Roald.

—*P. F.*

CONTENTS

IV The Expedition: Across Canada

BANKS ISLAND

ARCTIC OCEAN

BARROW

Smith Bay

Eskimo Islands

Beechey Point

Bullen

Brownlow Point

PRUDHOE BAY
DEADHORSE

KAKTOVIK

Camden Bay

Cache

Demarcation Bay

Beaufort Sea

King Point

Shingle Point

Harrowby Bay

Ice road on river

Amundsen Gulf

Smoking Hills

Cache at east side
of Albert Bay

Bar 1

TUKTOYAKTUK

Bear encounter
by Horton River

Nechilik ship

Hardin River

PAULATUK

Darnley Bay

ARCTIC NATIONAL
WILDLIFE
REFUGE

Colville River

ARCTIC CIRCLE

Mackenzie
River Delta

Yukon River

Porcupine River

ALASKA

USA
CANADA

FAIRBANKS

MOUNT
McKINLEY
(DENALI)

Great
Bear
Lake

YUKON
TERRITORY

Mackenzie River

NORTHWEST

TALKEETNA

Glenn Highway

TOK

2

ANCHORAGE

1

Alaska Highway

1

GULF OF

ALASKA

WHITEHORSE

1

Watson
Lake

Alaska Highway

FORT
NELSON

97

JUNEAU

BRITISH
COLUMBIA

DAWSON
CREEK

MILES

0   100   200   300

0   100   200   300   400

KILOMETERS

Direction of Travel

Dog Sled Route

Air Route

Railway Route

Highway Route

Highways

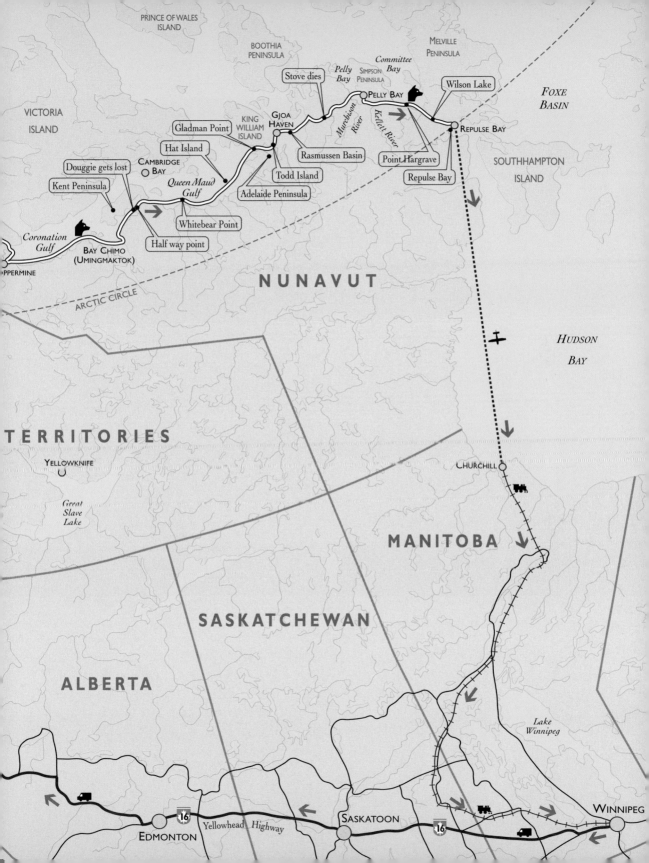

▲ *The tundra under cloudy skies.*

BEGINNINGS

✳

Doggie Dreams

DECEMBER 2, 1992

    We're on our way! Days of packing, weeks of training, months of planning, years of dreaming. Now it's all really happening. My dogs and I are flying from Anchorage to Prudhoe Bay. This has been such a big dream of mine for so long, the idea of actually getting started is almost overwhelming.

    As the plane lifted off, I didn't bother looking out the window. Instead, I closed my eyes and began daydreaming. A smile spread across my face. Soon I would be standing on the runners of my dogsled, skimming across the Arctic snow under a huge, blue sky sparkling with cold. No roads, no buildings, no other human beings would be in sight. Just my dogs and me, all alone.

    We'd already been to the Arctic several times on short adventures. I was returning because I loved it. Now I wanted to try a longer expedition, one that would allow us to stay, not for weeks, but months. The trip I had in mind would test all the dog mushing and survival skills I'd been working on for years.

    I'd decided to retrace an expedition taken in 1923–24 by Danish explorer Knud Rasmussen and two Inuit companions from Greenland, a man named Miteq and a woman named Anarulunguaq. Together the three traveled the entire length of the North American Arctic coast from east to west by dog team, from Repulse Bay, Canada, to Barrow, Alaska, a journey of 2,500 miles. If I accomplished the expedition, I would be the first female and first American to mush across the same route solo.

    Because I lived in Alaska, I decided to do the trip in reverse, starting in Barrow and traveling east through Canada. My dogs and I would cover the miles, about a hundred more than the distance between Seattle and New York, one paw at a time, powered only by our own muscles and wits. There would be no helicopter support, no photography crew, and no human traveling companions. I expected the trip would take three to six months to complete. It was the expedition of my dreams.

The desire to make this expedition didn't just appear suddenly, out of nowhere. When I look back, I can see it was part of a much larger dream that began when I was a kid growing up in Michigan.

I was eleven years old when a scientist came to my school to show slides and talk about Antarctica. I don't remember anything he said. But I clearly recall an image: a photograph of endless snow-covered mountains under a brilliant blue sky.

Immediately I knew I wanted to go to a place like that. The landscape was beautiful, so clean and empty. Best of all, there were no people. To a loner like me, it looked like the most perfect place imaginable.

Even back then, I spent most of my time alone. I didn't fit in well at school. My best friend was my dog, a German shepherd named Lady. Together we wandered the woods near my home, exploring for hours. I imagined ways we could survive in the wilderness—the food I would gather, the shelter I would build. I spent as many hours as possible outside with Lady.

I learned to love that time outdoors, alone with my dog. It became the source of my well-being. But I had no idea that someday I'd explore with my dogs for real in one of the harshest environments on Earth. I didn't expect to grow up to be an Arctic adventurer.

People are usually surprised to learn that a quiet, soft-spoken woman with glasses, who stands five feet tall and weighs just over a hundred pounds, is capable of mushing single-handedly through blizzards, ice, snow, and encounters with polar bears. In fact, I've been told all my life that I "couldn't" do many of the things I've done.

I have to admit, I've enjoyed proving people wrong.

Still, it's a long journey from a classroom in Michigan to a dogsled in the Arctic. How did I get there?

First I finished school and went on to college. In 1973 I began a career as a respiratory therapist in a hospital in Houston, Texas. To outward appearances, my life was moving along just fine. But there was one problem: I was very unhappy.

Something in my life felt wrong, but I couldn't put my finger on what it was. Finally, one day I happened upon a magazine article about a man named Naomi Uemura, a Japanese dog musher, mountaineer, and adventurer. While staring at one of the photographs of Uemura at the North Pole, standing alone in a vast snow-white wilderness, I remembered my old dream. It rushed over me like a full-blown blizzard.

I realized that I *hated* living in a big, hot city, surrounded by cars and pavement and buildings and people. I was about as far away from the snowy vastness I longed for as I could possibly get.

After some serious thought, I decided to quit my job and follow my dream. I was fortunate. My education had led to a well-paying job, so I'd been able to save quite a bit of money. In 1981, when I was thirty-five years old, I sold my belongings and used my savings to move to Alaska. There I planned to learn the wilderness skills I would someday need to take a dog-mushing journey to Antarctica. Call it escapism, call it denial, call it crazy—but I was determined to try. I figured I could always go back to my regular job.

In Willow, Alaska, I found the Howling Dog Farm, operated by Earl and Natalie Norris. They owned more than two hundred energetic sled dogs and generously allowed novices like me to live in their home. In return for room and board, I worked with their dogs, learning to care for and train huskies.

Howling Dog Farm was an exciting place. I'd never seen so many dogs in one spot before! The dogs were tethered to their own individual houses in the dog lot, which spread out over a couple acres like a sprawling canine subdivision.

Each musher on the farm was assigned a group of about twenty dogs to work with over the coming winter. All morning the dog lot was a hub of activity as team after team left to race around the trail system. Afternoons were spent cleaning the dog lot. It was a peaceful time, when I could think.

We were encouraged to pet the dogs and talk to them, from which I soon learned two things: petting a warm dog on a cold day really helps warm up your hands; and, just like humans, each dog is truly unique. Most dogs liked to be petted and talked to. Others liked to be talked to, but not petted. Some seemed indifferent to either. Best of all, every dog liked to sing. (Well, most people might call it *howling*, but in dog-mushing circles we call it singing!)

Evenings at Howling Dog Farm were spent feeding the dogs, eating dinner, and falling asleep shortly thereafter, usually over a book. The schedule was demanding, and the work hard, cold, and dirty, but I enjoyed it. Strong bonds of respect and affection developed between "my" dogs and me.

Gradually I learned about dog mushing. I took the dogs out on training runs, first for a few hours a day, then on overnight trips. I felt immensely proud as I watched them evolve into happy, hard-working teams.

In 1982, when my savings ran low, I began working part-time as a respiratory therapist in Anchorage, seventy miles away. I also built a small cabin in Willow near the Norrises and, with my remaining savings, bought five of the best dogs I'd worked with over the winter. I began breeding dogs to establish my own kennel. At first it was hard to leave the other fifteen dogs and my dog-mushing friends. I visited often but soon discovered that I truly enjoyed living alone with my dogs.

In 1983 I ran the 1,200-mile Iditarod Trail Sled Dog Race, not to win, but to learn about caring for dogs on long journeys. Over the next several years I launched two successful expeditions to the Magnetic North Pole and several along the northern coast of Alaska. Each time I learned more about dog mushing and wilderness survival. As my skills increased, so did my confidence. I also learned that I preferred to travel solo—just my dogs and me.

Between adventures I read everything I could about dogs and arctic history, culture, and exploration. I'd fallen in love with the Arctic and decided to stay in Alaska for the rest of my life. In 1990 the dogs and I moved farther north to a small log cabin near Talkeetna, about a hundred miles south of Mount McKinley, North America's tallest mountain.

By 1991 I'd been on seven expeditions, financed mostly with my own earnings but also some small contributions from friends and supporters. All the trips were fairly short, less than six weeks long. Each time I'd formed a close bond with my dogs and felt thoroughly at peace with myself. I never wanted the expeditions to end. Just like when I was a kid, I hated having to go home!

I finally felt confident enough to do something really big. One day, while reading Knud Rasmussen's book *Across Arctic America*, I hit upon the idea of retracing the expedition he had described. I began planning the journey, knowing full well that it would challenge every survival skill, every ounce of resolve and determination I possessed.

The original five dogs I'd purchased in 1982 had passed away by then. But they'd left me with puppies that had grown up to have puppies. Now my kennel consisted of eight beautiful, healthy, happy dogs: Douggie, Matt, Alice, Lucy, Sojo, Roald, Anna, and Robert.

In the summer of 1992 we started training long and hard around home. When there was no snow, the dogs pulled an ATV four-wheeler along gravel roads near my cabin. After snowfall they pulled a sled loaded with increasingly heavier weight. The dogs seemed to catch my determination. Every day they ran off happily for another day of training. As their feet and muscles toughened, so did their ability to work hard.

I also trained furiously. I cut and chopped firewood, hauled drinking water, lifted weights, walked five miles a day, shoveled snow, and dug dirt. I even got rid of every chair in my cabin. On the expedition I'd have to stand on the sled all day, so I figured I'd better get used to standing.

In the evenings I pored over every detail of every map again and again. I repaired dog harnesses, made lists, organized shipments of supplies, wrote letters to potential sponsors, reread *Across Arctic America*, and snatched a little sleep whenever I could.

After a year of preparation and training, one stubborn problem remained: it costs a lot of money to run an expedition—and I had almost none! I'd written hundreds of letters looking for sponsorship, hoping to find some companies interested in donating to the expedition. While a few companies helped with product donations, such as a camp stove, most said "No, thanks." Some never even answered my letters. Occasionally I actually got a foot in the door and met with someone about sponsorship, but was always turned down. One man told me he'd expected a large, aggressive woman. He was convinced, just by looking at me, that I had absolutely no chance of succeeding. Another man informed me that women had no business doing this sort of thing.

I learned that prejudice comes in many forms: wrong race, wrong color, wrong gender, too fat, too skinny, too tall, too small, too young, too old, too whatever. I was quickly becoming frustrated and angry. But I was not about to let go of my dream! I'd been on seven Arctic expeditions without ever losing a dog. I knew what I was doing and had earned the right to be taken seriously. I decided to channel my anger and frustration into energy to fuel my dream.

Still critically short on money, but long on enthusiasm, I borrowed from a friend the $18,000 I would need. It was scary to go so far into debt, but I believed in myself and my dogs.

Now, at last, we were headed north to begin two months of training in the Arctic. If the dogs proved they could handle the harsh conditions, the real expedition could begin. Step by step, mile by mile, we were moving closer to my dream.

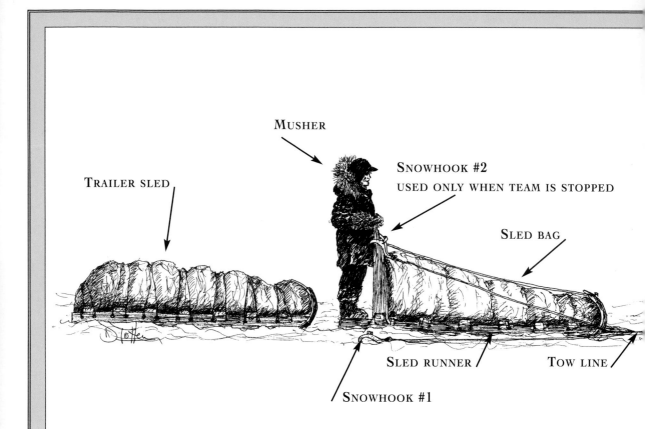

MUSHER

SNOWHOOK #2
USED ONLY WHEN TEAM IS STOPPED

TRAILER SLED

SLED BAG

SLED RUNNER

TOW LINE

SNOWHOOK #1

ILLUSTRATION © 2001 BY DAVID TOTTEN

Lead dogs: run in front position. They keep the other dogs in line and on the trail. The lead dogs follow commands from the musher: *all right* to go; *gee* to turn right; *haw* to turn left; and *whoa* to stop. As in any relationship, one lead dog is more assertive than the other and responds to commands more quickly. Good leaders work together, can often travel without a trail through darkness and blizzard, and seem to know if ice is too thin for crossing. Not every dog has the temperament to be a leader. Lead dogs are vitally important to the success of a dog team.

Swing dogs: work right behind the lead dogs and help swing the team in the correct direction on turns. Swing dogs often rotate into lead position for short periods (one or two hours) to give leaders a break.

Dogsled Team Positions

(Team on a rest break)

LEAD DOGS

WHEEL DOGS   TEAM DOGS   SWING DOGS

TUG LINE

HARNESS

SNOWHOOK #3
USED ONLY WHEN
TEAM IS ON A
REST BREAK

Team dogs: work behind swing dogs and in front of wheel dogs. No special responsibilities are required of team dogs, just a willingness to pull together with the other dogs.

Wheel dogs: work directly in front of the sled and help swing the sled on turns.

Musher: stands on the back of the sled runners or sometimes runs alongside the sled. She is the coach, or boss, of the team, giving the dogs commands so that they know where to go. The musher is also responsible for the care of the dogs, keeping them healthy, happy, and eager to run. ☾

Meet the Team

My dogs are Alaskan huskies, which is a mixed-breed dog with a double coat. The mix for my dogs is Siberian and Eskimo husky.

In many ways, a dog team is like a sports team. To be successful, each member must train physically. Everyone must learn to work together under the direction of a coach, with each individual contributing unique, important abilities to the team.

Early on, as I trained my dogs around our home near Talkeetna, I watched them closely. Each dog had to prove worthy and capable of being included on the rigorous expedition. I was also looking at the individual qualities of each dog to help me determine suitable team positions. In essence, they were "trying out" for the team.

These were the members of my mushing team:

▲ *Lead dog Douggie resting at midday.*

Douggie

AGE AT START OF EXPEDITION: 9 years.
SIZE AND COLORING: 75 pounds. Black.
PERSONALITY: Dependable, obedient, intelligent, confident, happy.
POSITION IN TEAM: #1 lead dog.
RELATIONSHIP TO OTHER DOGS: Father of Robert.
NAMED FOR: Douglas Mawson, an Antarctic explorer from Australia.
COMMENTS: Douggie was #1 lead dog because he wasn't afraid to stay out in front of the team and, most important, because he was obedient. I could always count on him to do what I commanded, unless, as sometimes happened, he knew better than I did! His good instincts and dedication saved our lives many times. Douggie had floppy ears that bounced as he walked.

Anna

AGE AT START OF EXPEDITION: 1 year.
SIZE AND COLORING: 45 pounds. Gray.
PERSONALITY: Confident, hard-working, happy, exuberant.
POSITION IN TEAM: #2 lead dog and sometimes swing dog.
RELATIONSHIP TO OTHER DOGS: Sister to Sojo and Roald. Daughter of Alice.
NAMED FOR: Anarulunguaq, an Inuit woman from Greenland who was the first known female explorer to cross the Arctic.

▲ *Anna eating a midday snack.*

COMMENTS: Anna always looked me straight in the eye. I wasn't sure she was mature enough for the trip, but her hard-working nature convinced me to let her try. Later I was thankful.

Alice

AGE AT START OF EXPEDITION: 6 years.
SIZE AND COLORING: 45 pounds. Gray.
PERSONALITY: Friendly, energetic, hard-working.
POSITION IN TEAM: Swing dog and occasional lead dog.
RELATIONSHIP TO OTHER DOGS: Mother of Sojo, Roald, and Anna.
NAMED FOR: Alice Paul, a suffragist who worked to win voting rights for women.

▲ *Alice asleep with Roald in the background.*

COMMENTS: Alice was an excellent mother, fun-loving but responsible. She often acted as playful as her puppies. Alice lacked the confidence to take commands directly, but she understood them and helped the leader swing the team.

Robert

▲ *Robert, with a red collar, ignoring me.*

AGE AT START OF EXPEDITION: 6 years.
SIZE AND COLORING: 65 pounds. Gray.
PERSONALITY: Charming, disobedient, friendly.
POSITION IN TEAM: Wheel dog.
RELATIONSHIP TO OTHER DOGS: Douggie's son. Father of Anna, Sojo, and Roald.
NAMED FOR: Robert Peary, a famous American explorer who claimed to be the first man to reach the North Pole.
COMMENTS: Robert was my only delinquent. He was never a leader because he never did anything he was told! But he was a charmer who loved people. He had a way of endearing himself that made it hard to stay angry with him for long and even harder to think about leaving him behind.

Sojo

▲ *Sojo on her back, waiting for a foot inspection.*

AGE AT START OF EXPEDITION: 1 year.
SIZE AND COLORING: 45 pounds. Black with white markings.
PERSONALITY: Extremely shy, hard-working, very sweet.
POSITION IN TEAM: Wheel dog and team dog.
RELATIONSHIP TO OTHER DOGS: Sister to Anna and Roald. Daughter of Alice.
NAMED FOR: Sojourner Truth, a courageous woman and freed slave who worked to abolish slavery.
COMMENTS: Sojo avoided eye contact and found it difficult to stand up for herself; yet she worked hard and had a sweet personality. She and Anna liked to cuddle when resting.

Roald

AGE AT START OF EXPEDITION: 1 year.
SIZE AND COLORING: 60 pounds.
  Gray and white pinto.
PERSONALITY: Happy, playful.
POSITION IN TEAM: Wheel dog and
  team dog.
RELATIONSHIP TO OTHER DOGS: Brother
  to Anna and Sojo. Son of Alice.
NAMED FOR: Roald Amundsen, a famous
  Norwegian explorer who led two
  important expeditions: the first to the South Pole and the first
  successful journey through the Northwest Passsage.
COMMENTS: Though intelligent, Roald lacked confidence, which
  sometimes caused him to clown around rather than try his
  hardest. But he was always cheerful, happy, and fun.

▲ *Roald thinking
happily about digging
in a seal hole.*

Lucy

AGE AT START OF EXPEDITION: 8 years.
SIZE AND COLORING: 45 pounds. Red
  and white.
PERSONALITY: Extremely shy, dependable,
  hard-working.
POSITION IN TEAM: Swing, wheel, and
  team dog.
RELATIONSHIP TO OTHER DOGS: Mother
  of Alice and Matt. Grandmother of
  Sojo, Roald, and Anna.
NAMED FOR: Lucy Burns, a suffragist.
COMMENTS: With Matt and Alice, Lucy formed the backbone of
  the team. She loved to be talked to, but not touched. With her
  reddish coat and small size, I nicknamed her "Foxy Lady."

▲ *Lucy.*

Matt

▲ *Matt, just outside Barrow, near sunset.*

AGE AT START OF EXPEDITION: 6 years.
SIZE AND COLORING: 65 pounds. Gray.
PERSONALITY: Hard-working, dependable.
POSITION IN TEAM: Swing dog.
RELATIONSHIP TO OTHER DOGS: Brother to Alice. Son of Lucy.
NAMED FOR: Matthew Henson, an African-American explorer who accompanied Robert Peary on all his expeditions.
COMMENTS: Choosing "Mighty Matt" was easy—he's the hardest-working dog I've ever known. He's also the only dog I've known who needed to diet during an expedition!

Pam Flowers

▲ *Pam, at the end of the trip in front of Repulse Bay.*

AGE AT START OF EXPEDITION: 46 years.
SIZE AND COLORING: 100 pounds. Straight, shoulder-length brown hair, hazel eyes.
PERSONALITY: Quiet, shy around people, persistent, determined, hard-working.
POSITION IN TEAM: Musher.
RELATIONSHIP TO DOGS: Coach, boss, "mother," partner, friend.
NAMED FOR: No one in particular.
COMMENTS: Pam loves being outdoors, especially on the back of a dogsled in the Arctic. She's very stubborn about achieving goals and hates to give up. ☾

II

TRAINING

✵

Prudhoe Base Camp

DECEMBER 3, 1992

I fed the dogs a light meal and set to work. The rest of the day was spent repackaging my personal food into daily rations and sorting some of my gear. The dogs and I are beginning to feel better after the stress-filled day of flying. Late in the evening, I gave the dogs a second, more generous meal to give them lots of extra water and calories. It's not terribly cold, -12°F with S/SE winds at about 15 miles per hour (m.p.h). But after the above-zero temperatures back home, it's relatively cold. The dogs will have to adjust. That means they need extra food to stay warm and to grow thicker coats.

When I stepped off the plane at Prudhoe Bay the sun had already set—not just for the day, but for the next six weeks. Darkness covered the land like a thick blanket quilted with stars. Within seconds, I felt the skin on my face tighten and sting from the dry, freezing air. My clothes stiffened and made a crinkly, scraping sound as I walked.

A friend, Jeff Veteto, had arranged for two workers he knew, Larry Eichmann and Paul Maloney, to meet us at the airport. I dug out my battery-powered headlamp and we got busy. Larry and Paul kindly transported us and all our gear to an empty shed owned by Catco, a heavy-equipment company that was allowing me to store my supplies. It took two big loads.

Prudhoe Bay is an enormous oil field on Alaska's North Slope. About forty miles wide, it is dotted with drill sites and crisscrossed by roads and pipelines. At the central camp, which is actually located in a town called Deadhorse, just a mile south of Prudhoe, numerous buildings house workers and machinery. It would serve as my base for the next two months of training.

■

The flight north had been exhausting—nine hours long, with stops at Fairbanks and Barrow. The dogs had been cooped up in their kennels the entire time. We were all bone-weary. I staked out the dogs in the shelter of some heavy equipment. Larry worried about the dogs sleeping outside in the cold, but I assured him that they were used to it. As long as I fed them well and protected them from the worst of the wind, they would be fine.

As soon as possible I pitched my tent beside the dogs, pushed in my sleeping mats and bag, and crawled inside. The tent would be my bed and bedroom throughout most of the next six months.

The next morning I set about finding the training supplies I'd sent up by parcel post two weeks earlier. Each day the dogs and I would need a mound of provisions: twenty pounds of dog food, two-and-a-half pounds of people food, and a half-gallon of gas for my little cook stove. Multiplied by the sixty days we'd spend training, that mound grew to a rather large mountain!

Even before I ate breakfast, I began soaking dry dog food in a five-gallon bucket full of hot water. This "dog porridge" helped me meet one of my

Food for the Trail

Whether canine or human, it takes a lot of calories to keep up your energy in the Arctic. Meals on the trail have to be high in calories, nutritious, and easy to prepare. The dogs ate a high-quality, nutritionally balanced dry dog food, the kind usually found in pet or feed stores, with occasional treats of meat or fish.

I chose foods that I liked enough to eat no matter how tired I was. For breakfast most days, I ate frozen, precooked summer sausage, cheese, and tea. Lunch was usually logan bread, a dense, slightly sweet loaf loaded with nutrition from whole grains, eggs, nuts, and fruits. Dinner consisted of frozen steak, rice, and frozen vegetables, which I cooked on my camp stove. Dessert was trail mix, hot chocolate, and tea before bed.

I packaged all my food in advance into one-day rations inside plastic freezer bags. Each morning on the trail, I simply pulled out one bag containing all my meals for that day.

I shipped as much food, portioned and packaged, to the villages along my route as I could ahead of time, including such items as cocoa mix, tea, trail mix, rice, the dry ingredients for logan bread, and dog food. Other items, such as steak, sausage, cheese, margarine, and the liquid ingredients for logan bread, I purchased along the way. Before leaving home I baked enough logan bread to last through training and the early part of the expedition. After that, I kept up my supply by baking the bread myself whenever I stopped in a village. Many people kindly allowed me use of their kitchens to do so. ◖

constant challenges: getting enough water into the dogs. Dehydration was always a concern in the Arctic, which is so dry it's actually a frozen desert. If the dogs didn't drink enough liquid, they would get sick. Yet dogs who live outside in winter—as all working sled dogs do—refuse to drink plain water during the cold months.

It would be impossible to carry enough food and fuel for our entire trip, so I decided to use our training time to cache supplies for part of the expedition. During training we would haul provisions to several spots along the first 200-mile section of our route. I tried to calculate the right amount of supplies needed to get us from one cache to the next. These caches became important training goals; delivering them would toughen us to arctic conditions, teach the dogs to run in wind and without trails, and help us come together as a team. Just as important, we would depend on the caches to survive once the expedition began.

DECEMBER 5, 1992   -10°F   15 M.P.H. S/SE

Plans to make our first training run today have been scrapped. When I went out to harness the dogs I found seven dogs and one collar. The collar belonged to Lucy, who loves to play keep-away whenever she gets loose. I didn't know how she got out of her collar, but I knew this was going to take time.

I tried in vain to catch her. She always stood at a right angle to the direction of my approach, with a look of total disinterest on her face. As I got to within three feet, she slowly and calmly moved away, just out of reach. It was infuriating, because I knew she knew exactly what she was doing. And I knew she was laughing at me!

I changed my strategy. I got my little shovel and small sled, used to clean the area and haul away droppings, and started scooping. I scooped closer and closer until I was standing right beside her. I thought, "I can get her now!" but as the thought went through my mind, Lucy, with that look still on her face, casually moved a few feet away.

We repeated the process over and over until finally Lucy turned her casual, disinterested little dog face away from me at a critical moment. I lunged for her and managed to grab her by the back legs as she made a last-second attempt to escape. I planted my head firmly against her furry behind and refused to let go. She resigned calmly to the fact that she was captured and surrendered without any fuss.

All the while, she kept that look on her face until I brought her some straw. Then she perked up, wagged her tail, and became very animated.

I gave her the straw as a way of calling a truce over our little battle, and making her life a little happier. This called for straw for everyone, to keep the peace.

So much for great expectations! By the time Lucy was finally captured, the three hours of dusk that signified midday were already fading rapidly. I didn't want to make our first training run in total darkness. Besides, the dogs were already bedded down contentedly in their fresh straw. I was disappointed to put off running one more day—but all the more determined that training would start tomorrow.

DECEMBER 6, 1992   -10°F   15 M.P.H. NE

Sometime during the night the wind shifted to the NE. I moved the empty dog kennels into a row in front of the dogs to make a windbreak as they had little protection from the NE wind. They liked that.

I took two teams out. First Doug, Robert, Lucy, and Roald. Next team, Matt, Alice, Sojo, and Anna. Both teams did well going out but had some trouble coming back. That's part of the reason we're up here training. The dogs must learn to run where there are no trails and get used to the constant wind and open spaces.

Back home we trained all fall and early winter. But there are dense forests surrounding the log cabin where I lived. We could only train on trails or on the infrequently traveled roads. The dogs didn't have to pay attention to where the trail was because there was only one place to go.

That evening I tried to glue and tape my glasses back together. Anna had accidently broken them when we'd returned from the second run that day. While I was unharnessing her she'd jumped up, wanting only to get her face up close to mine for a good lick. Unfortunately, she bumped off my glasses in her enthusiasm. I did my mending in the Catco crew's break room, where the light was better and the heat would help the glue to work.

Even though there were people around, they were usually working, and I was almost always alone. I was feeling increasingly lonely the longer we were stuck in camp. I desperately wanted to get out on the trail, where the dogs and I could really bond. Then I wouldn't feel so isolated.

DECEMBER 8, 1992   -12°F   22 M.P.H. NE, GUSTING PAST 30 M.P.H.

We stayed in camp again today. It's still too stormy outside. I can hardly see across the parking lot. I hope I haven't made a mistake by coming up here so early. But it's still good for the dogs because they'll get thicker coats and get used to the cold. The problem is that we're getting almost no training miles in. No use worrying about it, though; we're here, and that's all there is to it.

Two days of bad weather kept us in camp. The wind howled, blasting a steady supply of sharp, grainy snow sideways. It swirled and skittered across the ground in a frenzy. Visibility was about zero; I couldn't see ten feet in front of me.

We couldn't train, so I spent some time just sitting beside the dogs. It was good for us to get used to being together during a storm. Matt and Alice lay beside each other; I petted them and rubbed behind their ears. Then I talked to and petted all the others. The dogs didn't seem to mind the weather, especially if it meant some extra attention from me.

DECEMBER 9, 1992   -19°F   15 M.P.H. NE

The weather is starting to calm down, so I took two teams out today. I used the same line-up as before. Douggie is doing very well in lead, but his son, Robert, keeps goofing him up. Robert loves to visit and is forever trying to visit trucks we see moving along the ice roads. And he tries to chase birds flying overhead.

My sled handle broke while running the second team. The snow here is so hard that the sled takes a tremendous beating all the time. It's pretty exciting to be bouncing across the frozen tundra behind four healthy, strong dogs who love to run all out. But when the handle breaks and you have to try to balance with half a handle and not get bucked off, the feeling shifts slightly toward terror.

But I love it. This is what sledding in the Arctic is all about. I love taking risks I think I'm capable of handling.

I was really getting anxious to take our first overnight trip. Unfortunately, the weather wouldn't cooperate. Some days the temperature with the wind chill factor reached -75°F—cold enough to freeze spit in midair. Stepping into that cold, dry air made my face feel like it was being shrink-wrapped, as my muscles and skin contracted. Even my eyeballs felt dry and stinging from the cold.

Combined with blowing snow and whiteouts, it was simply too dangerous to move. The dogs, however, were thriving. Robert and Alice, Douggie and Roald, Anna and Sojo had quickly learned to cuddle up in pairs to share body heat.

It was hard, but I tried to remain patient. The weather would break and our chance would come. To pass the time I read books, talked to people, and

Temperature and Wind Chill

Each morning at about eight o'clock I recorded the temperature in degrees Fahrenheit, noted the direction from which the wind was blowing, and measured the speed, or force, of the wind with an instrument called an anemometer.

Wind increases the loss of body heat and causes the air to feel colder on exposed flesh than the actual temperature would indicate. I had to be careful to factor in the effect of wind chill in order to dress properly to prevent hypothermia and frostbite. As you can see from the chart below, at -40°F even a moderate fifteen-mile-per-hour wind causes the air to feel more than twice as cold. Wind chill below -20°F is considered extremely cold—so cold that in just one minute human flesh begins to freeze.

The wind chill index is calculated using a mathematical formula, which can be found at www.crh.noaa.gov, a website of the National Oceanic and Atmospheric Administration. This formula was recently revised. The following chart reflects the changes. ☾

Wind Chill Chart

Air Temperature in Degrees Fahrenheit								
	30	20	10	0	-10	-20	-30	-40
Wind Speed (m.p.h.)								
5	25	13	1	-11	-22	-34	-46	-57
10	21	9	-4	-16	-28	-41	-53	-66
15	19	6	-7	-19	-32	-45	-58	-71
20	17	4	-9	-22	-35	-48	-61	-74
25	16	3	-11	-24	-37	-51	-64	-78
30	15	1	-12	-26	-39	-53	-67	-80
35	14	0	-14	-27	-41	-55	-69	-82
40	13	-1	-15	-29	-43	-57	-71	-84

Source: National Weather Service, NOAA, U.S. Department of Commerce

prepared to lay out our first cache by calculating and bagging up the daily rations we would need. As soon as the weather improved, we'd be ready to head out toward Bullen, an abandoned radar station that was part of the Distant Early Warning system, or DEW Line as it was usually called. Bullen lay forty miles and at least two days away to the east.

First Training Run: Bullen

I knew that if a large, fully loaded sled got stuck, it would be too heavy for me to budge. But I could handle two smaller sleds. So rather than using one big sled, I chained two smaller, eight-foot sleds together. I call this my "brains over brawn" system.

The dogs ran in pairs, with each dog harnessed to a main rope called a gangline, which was attached to the front of the first sled. The second, or trailer, sled was tethered by a long rope to the first sled. I rode on the runners of the first sled. Two heavy, double-pronged, iron snowhooks were attached to the first sled by long ropes, one on each side of the sled. I used the snowhooks to anchor the sled securely from the rear, and sometimes fastened a third hook up front, attached behind the lead dog, as well.

The sleds were packed with enough supplies to last twelve days, including the cache items, plus our camping and cooking gear. Altogether, the load weighed about 620 pounds.

On December 15 we left for Bullen, our first extended trip. I hoped to make it there and back in about five days, but took rations for two extra days just in case. To help the dogs move the heavy load, I ran beside the sled a lot, or did what dog mushers call pedaling, pushing off with one leg to help move the sled along. The exercise helped me stay warm.

The land we traveled over was almost completely flat, with occasional soft, rounded hills that seldom reached more than ten feet high. Here, as we would do during much of the journey, we alternated between sledding over sea ice, along the shore of the bay, and taking shortcuts across points of land. Frozen creeks and rivers, which all flowed north in the summer, creased the soft, white landscape. Snow cover was thin and crusty, seldom more than six inches deep.

On the way we were forced to wait out several storms. I would sit alone in my little red-and-white tent, huddled fully clothed in my sleeping bag, listening to ice crystals beating against the walls and wind heaving the fabric. I wasn't worried about survival; the tent was specially designed and

▼ *Looking out of my tent, at a camp just before the Canadian border.*

constructed to handle the stresses of high winds. But after a while I got pretty bored.

My tent had a vent at the top, so I could run my camp stove without fear of toxic fumes from the fuel. Often during these storms I cooked up a batch of dog pizza. But before you start imagining dog chow with tomato sauce and cheese, let me explain!

Recipe for Dog Pizza

Make two batches of porridge (twenty pounds of dry dog food plus eight gallons of warm water) for the dogs' dinner. Feed half at dinner time. Keep one-quarter inside the tent, where it won't freeze, for their breakfast. Dump the remaining quarter out on the snow, behind the tent, where the dogs can't reach it. To make pizzas, press the porridge flat with the bottom of a dog bowl until it looks like a large pizza and let it freeze overnight. The next morning, there it is: dog pizza! Break into "slices" with a hatchet.

Just like humans, dogs love "pizza" at snack time.

Finally the storm broke and we continued. When we reached Bullen five days later, on December 20, I was thrilled. The dogs had run well without trails, through the wind, and we were all adjusting to the cold. Our first training goal was accomplished! I turned around and looked at my team, already curled up into little furry balls. "Hey, you wild dogs!" I called out. "It's time to celebrate!"

▼ The team resting and thinking about dinner while I set up camp.

I let every one of the dogs loose. While they tore about, gleefully playing tag in the deserted compound of four dilapitated Army buildings, I cached 100 pounds of dog food, a gallon of fuel, and five days of people food for our expedition on top of an old rusty boiler in an abandoned building. The dogs didn't settle down until dinner time.

The next day, December 21, it stormed all day. Still, I was happy because it was the shortest day of the year. That meant light would start increasing a little each day.

It stormed again the next day, and the next and next. Finally, on Christmas Eve day, the weather changed. It stopped snowing, and the temperature dropped to 34°F, not counting wind chill. We were getting short of food, so despite the cold, I decided to try to make it back to Prudhoe. Otherwise we'd be forced to start eating up our expedition cache.

Though the dogs didn't seem to mind, to me it felt brutally cold heading into the wind. I wore a neoprene face mask to keep my face from freezing, but had to stand sideways on the sled with my shoulder hunched to protect the corners of my eyes. In wind that cold, skin freezes almost instantly. I couldn't see anything because my glasses were in my pocket. Even frost-free glasses frost up below -25°F.

After three-and-a-half hours, despite two layers of long underwear, pants, shirt, sweater, snowpants, hooded parka, expedition beaver-fur mitts with two pairs of gloves inside, face mask, and a thick hat, I felt the cold creeping deep into my body. Inside my mitts, my fingers ached and stung. No matter how hard I pedaled, I couldn't warm up. That was a bad sign. It meant the start of hypothermia.

It was Christmas Eve. Across the flat tundra I could see the lights of Prudhoe Bay, with its warm buildings, holiday

Pam Flowers Arctic Expedition Camping Routine

- First, empty both sleds.

- Next, set up the tent. Stow camp stove, sleeping mats, sleeping bag, daily food ration, cooking utensils, and personal gear inside. Leave the shotgun outside the tent door, where it will be handy if needed to fend off marauding polar bears, but will stay free from the condensation that occurs inside the tent, which could cause misfiring.

- Pile dog food, extra people food, and fuel under the blue tarp. Weight down the tarp with fuel containers.

- Flip the empty sleds on their sides, end-to-end, to create a windbreak for the dogs. To picket the dogs behind the sleds, disconnect each dog's tug line from the harness, remove the harness, and attach the tug line to the dog's collar.

- While inspecting the dogs for harness rub or sore feet, touch them and talk in a soft, loving voice. Tell them what great dogs they are, how much they are loved, and how good-looking they are. (They especially love to be told they're good-looking.)

- To start dinner, carve blocks of snow with a keyhole saw and place them by the tent door. Inside the tent, on the two-burner camp stove, melt the blocks into water in a big pot. When four gallons of hot water are ready, pour in dry dog food. While the dog food soaks, cook and eat my own meal: steak, rice, frozen vegetables, decaf tea, and hot chocolate.

- Feed the dogs. While setting down each bowl, say the dog's name so that everyone knows whose bowl it is. (They are too well-mannered to fight over or steal food.)

- When the dogs finish eating, store the empty bowls under the tarp and make four more gallons of water for the next batch of dog food.

- While the snow melts, calculate the distance traveled that day, using the GPS navigator and maps. Write in the journal, drink more tea, and eat dessert, a trail mix of dried fruits, nuts, and candy.

- When the dog food is ready, pour out half for dog pizza. The rest, which is tomorrow's breakfast, stays in the tent so it doesn't freeze.

- Finally, if able to stay awake, read a few pages of a paperback novel. But more often, fall asleep, exhausted. ☾

dinners, and friendly people. But Prudhoe Bay lay nineteen long miles away. I felt too tired and numb to care about anything except warming up immediately. Rather than risk freezing to death, I stopped. Straining to work my stiff fingers on the tent and harnesses, I set up camp and tended to the dogs. Once inside the tent, my hands burned as they slowly warmed up.

On Christmas Day we set out again, this time in blinding snow. My glasses kept fogging up and freezing over, so I mostly relied on Douggie to find the way. I was exhausted and relieved when we pulled safely into Prudhoe Bay.

After taking care of the dogs, I eagerly accepted an invitation to a hot shower and Christmas dinner at one of the dining halls. Giant prawns, carrots, broccoli, fresh salad, cake, with plenty of water and juice, tasted heavenly. It felt marvelous to be completely warm, full of delicious food, and able to talk with someone besides myself!

I felt so pleased with our success that I gave myself a Christmas present: one night's sleep in a heated room. I moved my sleeping bag into the workers' lounge. All night long, even as I dreamed, I basked in warmth and contentment.

Second Training Run: Point Brownlow

On December 29 we set out to leave a second expedition cache at Point Brownlow, which lay eighty miles east, forty miles beyond Bullen. The dogs made much better time on this run because temperatures were warmer and they were getting used to the Arctic.

Two days later, on New Year's Eve, we were almost halfway there—and less than three miles from Bullen—when a tremendous storm roared toward us across the tundra. I could see it coming and had to make a quick decision. Should I put up the tent and bear the blast out in the open? Or race against the storm for the sheltering buildings at Bullen?

It was a tough call. If we tried and failed, it would be nearly impossible to set up the tent in the midst of the storm. Trying to survive a blizzard without a tent was not a pleasant thought.

Still, only three miles. I decided to make a run for it.

DECEMBER 31, 1992

The wind kept picking up, and soon the dogs' tails were pointing straight left while their heads pointed right toward the storm. Douggie knew

where we were heading and knew why we needed to get there. He maintained a brisk pace, but it wasn't fast enough. With just a half-mile to go, Bullen suddenly disappeared in a swirling chaos of white. All I could do was trust that Douggie would keep us on the right heading.

The blowing snow stung my eyes, and the sled kept slewing off to the left. The wind seemed to suck the breath right out of my lungs. I could barely make out the dogs as their coats were becoming covered with thick layers of snow. We seemed to go on for an eternity like that. I became convinced that we must have bypassed Bullen.

As if by magic, Bullen appeared out of the storm. The dogs went on their own to the exact spot where we'd camped the last time we were here.

From our sheltered camp, the tundra was a nightmare of snow blowing sideways. I was very happy to be here and not out there. I was also glad I had Douggie for a lead dog.

What a way to celebrate New Year's Eve!

For three days I waited out the raging weather. While the wind howled outside, battering my tiny shelter with gale-force winds, I wrote in my journal, tended the dogs, munched trail mix, and read paperback novels (usually westerns by Louis L'Amour). I also found myself thinking about Anarulunguaq, the Inuit woman who accompanied Rasmussen on his expedition.

▲ Anarulunguaq, the young Greenland Native woman who accompanied Knud Rasmussen and her cousin, Miteq, across Arctic America in 1923-24.

Although few people have heard of her, Anarulunguaq must have been an amazing woman. As far as I can determine, she was the world's first female Arctic explorer on record. When she, Rasmussen, and her cousin Miteq left from Repulse Bay, Canada, in March 1923 to travel across the top of North America, little was known by outsiders about the region. Anarulunguaq drove the dog teams, acted as an interpreter, and helped Rasmussen gather information about the history and culture of Inuit people in Canada and Alaska. She also cooked, mended, and sewed the fur clothing they needed to keep warm for survival. Miteq's main job was to hunt so they would have food along the way.

After thirteen months, the dogsled portion of their journey ended in Barrow, Alaska. Then, as now, it was rare for a woman to undertake a long journey of exploration in the Arctic. Although little is known about Anarulunguaq, I felt a connection to this brave and hardy woman. Was she drawn toward adventure, as I am? Did she endure ridicule, discouragement, or suspicion from others? Surely she experienced the same exhaustion, the deadly cold, the blizzards—and the joy—of travel by dogsled.

It was exciting to think I'd be visiting the same places Anarulunguaq had seen seventy years earlier. Of course, the Arctic has changed considerably in that time. Some adjustments had to be made. In our modern world of dwindling wildlife and strict hunting regulations, I wouldn't hunt to feed myself and my dogs. I would carry

Storm Warnings

If I paid attention to the warning signs, I could always tell when a storm was coming. The sky in the direction of an approaching storm would turn gray down to the horizon. If the advancing weather was simply windy, with no blizzard involved, I would see a thin blue line along the horizon. A storm could come from any direction, but the worst ones usually blew in from the east.

The dogs assisted me in reading the weather. They could hear a bad storm moving toward us before I could see it. If they kept looking off in the same direction, it usually meant a storm was on its way. This was especially helpful on days when cloudy weather had already turned the entire sky gray. Many times their advance warning enabled me to set up camp before a full-force blizzard hit. ☾

some of our provisions, arranging to pick up new supplies at our caches and in villages along the way. I didn't wear fur clothing, but cotton, wool, and synthetics. My equipment was a combination of high-tech stuff unimaginable to Anarulunguaq and Rasmussen, such as a GPS (global positioning system), or satellite navigator, as well as low-tech gear, such as an ice probe, which they too would have carried. Our method of travel—dogs pulling wooden sleds over ice and snow—was ancient.

To honor the first known female Arctic explorer, I decided to name my expedition "In the Tracks of Anarulunguaq." If I was successful, I hoped to gain recognition for Anarulunguaq, in particular, and female adventurers in general. I hoped that my example would encourage others, just as the example of her hardy spirit strengthened me.

As I bided time in my little tent, waiting for an end to what seemed a ceaseless battering by wind and snow, it was comforting to know that Anarulunguaq and others before me had endured similar blizzards. It was simply part of travel in the Arctic. This storm, like all others, would pass.

And finally, it did. On the fourth day, January 4, we could travel.

After being cooped up for days, it felt great to be moving. The dogs were eager and full of energy, running the first eighteen miles in only three hours. Then, as we neared Point Brownlow, we hit some rough sea ice and slowed to a crawl. Jumbled pieces of broken ice about three feet across and six inches thick, like slabs of demolished concrete, lay piled in every direction. After just a few feet of progress, one of the sleds would get stuck and we'd all jerk to a halt. Over and over I freed the sleds, we moved a few feet, and stuck fast again. The stopping and starting was tough on the dogs.

About three miles from Point Brownlow, a sled jammed tight beneath a large chunk of ice. I was exhausted and ready to give up right there.

Just then the dogs looked back at me, their little doggie faces inquisitive. I could swear they were asking, "What's the problem?"

Suddenly it hit me. They were doing their part—and counting on me to do mine! After all, we were a team.

I bent my back one more time and gave a mighty yank, and the sled broke free.

I was glad I did. Just a few minutes later we broke out of the rubble onto a lagoon with flat, solid ice. A few minutes more, and we were at Point Brownlow.

After placing our cache and resting a day, we practically flew back to Prudhoe in only two days. That proved to be very fortunate, because blizzards and extreme cold prevented training most days during the next two weeks.

When the sun returned to the sky on January 18, it appeared as a dim globe through a haze of snow. It skidded along the horizon for about an hour before setting. Still, it was a cheerful event. Each day now the sun would stay in the sky a few minutes longer, making life that much easier. By April it would be light all the time.

I was pleased with the dogs. They'd done well on both runs and were coming together as a team. They were a hard-working, happy crew, full of energy and the love of running.

Still, I knew there were weaknesses. And if there's one thing I'm good at, it's worrying. I worried because Sojo, Roald, and Anna were barely a year old. Could they hold up under the harsh conditions of Arctic mushing? I worried about Douggie. Although not yet too old, he was nearing the end of his prime. And what if he became sick or injured? I had no other reliable leader.

I harbored hopes that Anna might develop into a lead dog, but it was too soon to be sure. Without a leader, we simply couldn't run.

Despite my worries, I had a good feeling about this team. All of them showed tremendous enthusiasm for running. I knew from my own experience that intelligence, desire, and dedication can be far more important than age, size, and muscles.

I used the days in camp at Prudhoe to organize our final, and toughest, training run: 220 miles northwest to Barrow. If we did well, as I hoped and believed we could, the official expedition would begin there.

Final Training Run: Barrow

JANUARY 19, 1993   -43°F   10–25 M.P.H. W/SW
> I feel really antsy now and want to get this trip under way.

Once again it was too cold and windy for travel. I was sick and tired of being stuck in camp! There was nothing I could do about it except complain. Then I remembered it was a special day. Today Anna, Sojo, and Roald all turned one year old.

They were big dogs now! We celebrated with hamburgers for everyone. As I passed out patties of fried meat, I wished the trio "happy birthday" and told them how proud I was of their accomplishments.

I'm not sure they paid much attention to my words. They were too busy bolting down their burgers. As they sniffed through the snow for any dropped morsels, their wagging tails told me they appreciated their birthday party.

JANUARY 20, 21, 22, 23, 1993
> The weather has been nasty, but it's getting better. I've sorted and inventoried my gear and supplies. The dogs and I are all ready to go.

Winter blizzards are to be expected in the Arctic; still, people were saying it was an especially stormy year. I knew the severe cold would slow our pace, too. It not only sapped our energy, but also significantly increased the drag against sled runners, as it caused the millions of ice crystals to contract and become pointier. I began to think I'd better leave some extra caches between Barrow and Prudhoe so we wouldn't run out of food when we came back through on the expedition.

When the weather finally cleared on January 24, we left the Prudhoe base camp on our final training run. With help from Bill Kuper and other friends in trucks, I set one giant cache near the Colville River, off the ice road leading to Barrow. Then I headed west, alone, to Eskimo Islands, where I left another cache. The terrain in these areas reminded me of Midwest fields, with gentle, rolling hills as far as the eye could see. Tufts of tundra grass poked through the shallow snow. I wouldn't have been surprised to see cattle grazing.

On January 28 the dogs and I returned to the Colville cache, where I picked up enough supplies to make it to Barrow (I hoped) on this final training run. If all went well, we'd come back to the cache during the expedition to pick up the remaining three days' food and fuel.

JANUARY 28, 1993   -45°F   0–5 M.P.H.   NE   CLEAR

When we left the cache, the sled was heavier by about 180 pounds of dog food, fuel, and people food. We traveled an hour and forty minutes but still managed to make six-and-a-half miles before I set up camp. I was surprised that the dogs did so well with all that weight. They did get a one-and-a-half hour break while I was sorting the cache, so maybe that was the secret.

I used booties on Douggie, Matt, and Anna today. The booties help protect the dogs' feet when they get chafed or cut. The snow is so coarse and grainy when it is this cold. When I noticed their pads were getting a little worn, I put on the booties.

Anna had never worn booties before. I expected she would try to remove them like most young dogs do but she just left them on. Anna is developing faster than her siblings, Roald and Sojo, and seems to be a special sort of dog.

JANUARY 29, 30, 31, 1993   -24°F TO -45°F   25 M.P.H.   SW   STORM

Stormed for three days. When the storm started coming toward us, I flipped both sleds on their sides to make a shelter for the dogs. They liked being picketed together behind the sleds, where they could share their body heat.

During the storm I heard a strange noise and looked outside to see what was going on. The puppies were playing with each other and didn't seem to even notice the storm. Here I'd spent all this time worrying about them and they were playing! These dogs are tough.

Training

FEBRUARY 1, 1993   -36°F   15 M.P.H. SW   CLEAR

It took forever to dig out from the storm. I was worn out before we even got started. This seemed like the longest day in the saddle so far. It was so brutally cold that my face and hands stung and burned all day. I had to keep checking the dogs to make sure they weren't freezing up. We all got through the day OK, but it sure was cold.

FEBRUARY 2, 1993   -34°F   20–25 M.P.H. SW   BLOWING SNOW

Last night just before sundown, I watched the sun disappear behind a haze of clouds. Up here that is the ominous foretelling of a storm. Sure enough, when I woke up this morning it was blowing snow, poor visibility, and powerful headwinds. I am sick of these never-ending storms.

I know there are a lot of storms this time of year, but this is really starting to get to me. If it keeps up like this, we'll never finish.

Finally, on February 3, we reached the cache I'd set earlier at Eskimo Island. So far, we were doing fine with supplies. But if it kept storming, I was afraid we'd run really tight before reaching Barrow.

FEBRUARY 4, 1993   -46°F   5 M.P.H. SW   CLEAR

We traveled eighteen-and-a-half miles today. The dogs wanted to stop before I was ready, so I walked the last twenty minutes in front of them. They were willing to go on with me in front. The cold sapped all our strength and we finally stopped for the night.

FEBRUARY 5, 1993   -30°F   35–50 M.P.H. NE

I woke up in the night and the wind was really picking up, so I got out and checked the dogs. I moved the sleds to a different angle to give the dogs better protection.

By noon the storm was raging. It's the worst storm so far this year. When I look outside the tent, it looks like we're in a big mixing bowl and someone is beating egg whites really fast. The snow streaks by at tremendous speed.

By midafternoon the snow piling up behind the sleds was so high that the dogs were sleeping almost even with the tops of the sleds. So I got out my little shovel and crawled along on my knees, shoveling them out. As I moved along, each dog would lie down in the new trench behind me, grateful to be out of the full brunt of the wind.

It is a painful process for me. No matter how I try to shield my face, I can't keep snow from blowing into my eyes. The snow plasters itself in big clumps over my eyelids and along the sides of my face above my face mask. My eyelashes freeze together and I can't open my eyes. I have to crawl back to the tent on my knees, feeling my way along. I scramble into the tent and frantically claw the snow away from my eyes. It's painful to pull the frozen snow off my eyelashes, but it is freezing the skin of my eyelids.

Every three hours, round the clock, I repeat the procedure.

In the Arctic, the enemy is not so much the cold as the wind. In weather like that, it would have been easiest to stay inside the tent during the storm. But I care for my dogs no matter what the weather is, because I love them and want them to be safe. Though it's not much fun for me, it's worth it. I've never had a dog die on my expeditions.

Over and over, I told myself to be patient and careful. Impatience leads to poor judgment. In the Arctic, poor judgment leads easily to death. In weather like this, I could afford no mistakes.

FEBRUARY 6, 1993   -10°F   20 M.P.H. NE

I am exhausted from lack of sleep, but we have to travel. We can't afford another bitter storm if we are to reach Barrow before we run out of supplies.

The camp was badly drifted over. It took me three hours to dig out. The frostnip around my eyes was painful in the cold wind. At least it took my mind off my cold hands.

Amazingly, we did thirteen miles in just under three hours. Barrow is now ninety-five miles away. I should start seeing the lights glowing against the sky soon. That will be a warm sight to my cold eyes.

FEBRUARY 8, 1993   -2°F   15 M.P.H. SE

It has warmed up and the wind is behind us. We made twenty-nine miles. Barrow is just forty-one miles away!

FEBRUARY 9, 1993   -2°F   20 M.P.H. SW

About an hour after we got started, I found a snowmobile trail that seemed to be going in the right direction, so I got on it. I could see Douggie relax almost instantly. His floppy ears flopped even more than usual. He just kept his head down and sniffed along to keep us on the trail. Finding a way over the tundra and ice requires endless decision-making all day for a lead dog. It's mentally exhausting. I know he's really happy to find a trail.

About noon, the storm I feared overtook us. But it was warm, and because there was a trail we kept going. After an hour, it got too bad to continue. We stopped and snuggled down behind the sleds for an hour to escape the blowing snow.

I knew we'd made excellent time and thought about making camp. But I was concerned that the trail would be totally obscured by blowing snow during the night. It was getting warmer all the time, so I decided to go for it.

We kept moving steadily, with regular breaks. Then, as darkness fell, I saw a flashing light several miles ahead. I knew it had to be Barrow! Sometime later the dogs also saw it. It was like horses heading for the barn at the end of the day. There was no stopping us. I fed out some dry dog food and off we went.

By ten-thirty that night we were on the outskirts of Barrow. Though I knew that the population of the town was only five thousand, to me it looked like a huge city. I stopped and pitched camp for the night, feeling quite pleased.

A major goal had been achieved. We'd reached Barrow, our farthest and final training destination, in good shape and with food to spare. In fourteen days we'd covered 220 miles—an average of more than fifteen miles per day, despite extreme cold and numerous storm days. Not only that, we'd traveled forty-one miles in a single day!

Training was over. It was time to make a final decision: were we ready for the real expedition?

Though I still had a trio of youngsters, no sponsors, and no spare lead dog, I felt optimistic. We'd made it through several hundred miles of blizzards, cold, and heavy loads. Douggie was doing an excellent job as leader, Anna looked promising as a potential leader, and the team was working well together. With a little luck, and a lot of hard work, I had a gut feeling we could achieve our goal.

My dream, I decided, was truly within reach. It was time to follow in the tracks of Anarulunguaq. ☾

THE EXPEDITION: ACROSS ALASKA

Dog Singing

The expedition officially began on Valentine's Day, 1993, under a cloudless blue dome of sky. If we succeeded, our adventure would be entered in the record books. If we failed—well, who would care? Only I and a few disappointed friends.

No matter what, I told myself, we'd have an incredible experience few people can even imagine. It was the best Valentine's Day gift I could hope for.

The first leg of our trip would take us back to Prudhoe. But first we had to get out of town. I knew from experience that dog teams have a knack for embarrassing their drivers whenever other people are around. To reach the tundra, about one hundred yards away from my friend Craig George's house, we had to cross a road. If the dogs decided to goof around for the small crowd of well-wishers that had gathered, they might turn onto the road and drag me straight through downtown Barrow.

Craig came to the rescue. "Would you mind if Geoff and I ride over to the tundra with you?"

Would I mind? I wanted to hug him! Craig and his friend, Geoff Carroll, were both seasoned dog handlers. If the dogs misbehaved, Craig and Geoff could help me keep them under control.

I stood on the runners of the front sled; Craig and Geoff sat on the trailer sled. At 2:00 P.M. I lifted the snowhook and squeaked out a command: "All right, Douggie, let's go."

Without so much as a woof, Douggie led us across Craig's backyard, past a snowmobile, between two houses, around the neighbor's garage, down a driveway to the road, across the road, across a field, and around a telephone pole. Then he turned right and headed for Repulse Bay.

I felt foolish for having doubted him. Obviously, he knew exactly what he was doing and didn't need a bit of help, thank you very much! I made a mental note to make it up to him later.

Craig and Geoff jumped off and waved good-bye. With that, we were on our way.

FEBRUARY 14, 1993   -5°F 10 M.P.H. E 28 MILES

The sun was shining and it was a beautiful day. I thought I would feel excited, but for some reason I felt very subdued. Maybe because we'd already sledded so many miles.

As the miles rolled by, I started to relax and feel happy. A growing sense of excitement started to creep into my mind. We were actually beginning our trip! It was really happening.

I felt so happy that I wanted to sing "On the Road Again" (more famously sung by Willie Nelson) at the top of my lungs. Instead, I hummed quietly to myself. My dogs would bear almost any hardship—except my singing. If I sang, they refused to run!

For the first few miles the land was flat tundra, a treeless plain covered with ponds, lakes, and swamps. Gentle rolling hills, only a few feet high, reached over the horizon. As in most places in the Arctic, the snow cover was wind-packed and scant, with gravel, small boulders, and tufts of mossy plants poking through. To some people this part of the world is boring. But I love it. To me the Arctic has a stark, mesmerizing beauty.

We were lucky to have a smooth trail to follow that first day, which allowed us to cover twenty-eight miles in three-and-a-half hours. The second day we left the tundra, climbing over a bluff and then dropping down to the coastline. When I looked out over the frozen Arctic Ocean, I couldn't help thinking about the tremendous forces of nature at work here: the sun, with power to renew light and life, or in its absence, plunge the land into darkness; the cold, able to freeze an entire ocean; and the weather, covering the earth with snow. Yet all those substances were made of the same molecules as I was. I, too, was part of the nature all around me, and part of the energy that had made everything I was seeing. Just thinking about it filled me with a sense of power so overwhelming that I felt as if I could do anything.

Here was a world in which I felt at home. What other people thought of me didn't matter. Money problems didn't matter. There were no fences, no boundaries, no artificial rules to hold me back. If I paid attention to the environment and used common sense and my survival skills, I knew that we would be all right. No matter what.

By evening the next day, we reached Smith Bay, fifty-five miles from Barrow. The next day was spent sitting out a storm. For once, I didn't mind the delay. I'd picked up some cold germs in Barrow, which developed into a miserable chest cold. The forced rest helped me recover.

When we headed south to Teshekpuk Lake, I tried running Anna in lead with Douggie to see how she would do. The land grew progressively hillier until we reached a steep bluff at the edge of the lake.

FEBRUARY 17, 1993   +2°F   12 M.P.H.   36 MILES

As we dashed out onto the lake and started to turn left, Anna got mixed up and wanted to go right for some reason. Poor Douggie! He's had to run with her in lead most of the day. She doesn't know any commands yet, but she has to have a chance to learn. I think she has the most potential of any of the puppies. Her mistakes are exasperating to Douggie, who has to not only follow commands but correct her as well. But he is generally a patient teacher.

Some lead dogs might snarl or nip at the ear of a teammate if the teammate doesn't understand a command. Some lead dogs even refuse to run next to a beginner. But not Douggie. He would nudge Anna gently to the right on *gee* or tug her gently to the left on *haw* to teach her.

FEBRUARY 18, 1993   +10°F   LIGHT WINDS   38 MILES

The weather today was pleasant, but the heat is causing a whiteout. All day Douggie had to lead us through ice fog. It was so white that, at one point, when I stepped off the sled during a rest break, I nearly fell over as I looked away and across the tundra. The sled gives me some reference to keep my balance. But when I look away, there is nothing, and I can't tell up from down. There is absolutely no horizon.

I walked to the front of the team and looked out at what Douggie had to head into, and I didn't see how he does it. In one respect Douggie is the most amazing dog I've ever had for a leader. Each morning before we leave, I take a compass heading. Then, with the rear snowhooks firmly in place, I walk backward away from Douggie in the direction I want him to go. As I walk away from him, I clap my hands and call his name. He knows he can't come to me and just woofs at me. Then, I get on the sled, lift the hooks, and tell him to go. He follows the course I set for him all day, until I tell him to change. It's an incredible ability.

▼ The team by a cache at Eskimo Islands, as we headed east from Barrow on the actual expedition.

Later that day I noticed something that turned my stomach upside down: wolf tracks. I bent down to inspect them. The edges of the tracks were still clearly defined and the little ridges of snow in the middle of the tracks still soft. These tracks were fresh.

I'd heard that a large, black wolf lived in the area. With a dog team I'm more afraid of wolves than polar bears. A bear will usually keep clear of a dog team, but a wolf may walk right into camp and try to kill a dog in an attempt to protect its territory.

We were traveling through an area of rolling hills. Tonight, rather than camp in a depression, out of the wind, I decided to follow advice given to me by an Inuit hunter: always camp in the open, where you can see as far as possible in all directions. That way a predator has a hard time sneaking up on you.

We made it through the night without any wolf problems, but the next day brought total whiteout again. I knew from my map that we were near the Eskimo Island cache. In that fog it would be easy to miss, even for Douggie. We needed those supplies to make it to the Colville River cache.

FEBRUARY 19, 1993   +20°F   15 M.P.H. SW   34 MILES

The terrain seemed hillier than I remembered it. After a while I became convinced that we were going too far south. I tried to correct Douggie's

heading and get him moving more toward the north. Each time I called "Haw," he would swing north and then immediately swing back to the right. Over and over, I gave him the same command, and, over and over, he did the same thing. He simply ignored me and kept going his way. The longer he disobeyed me, the angrier I became.

I was determined to somehow get things back under control when we crested a high hill. There, about a hundred yards ahead, were all those posts sticking up out of the ground that marked our cache site.

I'll never understand how that dog can run through miles of mist and somehow take me exactly where I want to go. What is more baffling is that he often does it in spite of me! Sometimes I think, if I could just teach him how to melt snow into water, I could stay home and send Douggie out there to lead the team by himself.

We sledded up to the cache and I walked up to Douggie, who looked at me and wagged his tail. I kneeled down beside him, gave him a big hug, and apologized for yelling at him. Douggie woofed and gave me a big, sloppy kiss over my entire face, which was powerful enough to knock me over. Anna thought that was funny and started barking and bouncing around. Soon everyone was barking excitedly and wagging their tails. Then they all started to sing; more correctly, they started to howl in unison. I stood up, threw my head back, and howled with them. We were a team again, and everyone was happy.

The dogs don't mind if I sing their way!

Big, Black, Furry Wolf

Two days later we reached the Colville River cache. I could see the lights of Prudhoe Bay reflected in the sky at night and noticed an acrid odor from the oil fields. Though the aroma of civilization was unpleasant, I couldn't wait to reach Prudhoe. I found myself thinking constantly about food: pancakes, syrup, bacon, apple pie. A steady diet of trail rations was getting to me. I promised myself a hearty meal as soon as we arrived.

In a thick fog we approached Beechey Point, the site of an old, abandoned trading post. As we approached the weather-beaten building, a slight motion caught my eye.

FEBRUARY 22, 1993   -10°F   10 M.P.H. SW   41 MILES

I saw a black, furry rump disappear behind the right front corner of the trading post. The dogs saw it, too, and started lunging and barking furiously.

I felt panicky as I jammed both rear snowhooks into the snow. I snatched the third hook out of the sled bag and raced up to the front of the team and anchored them. The dogs were suddenly and strangely quiet already, but every eye was straining for a glimpse of whatever it was that was hiding behind the cabin.

I pulled the shotgun out, pumped a slug into the chamber, and flipped off the safety. The last thing I wanted was to confront a wolf. I was scared to go along the front of the building and lose sight of the team because I thought the wolf might be circling around the other side so it could attack my dogs. I faced the building and moved quickly to my right twelve steps. Then I saw black fur sticking out from beside the other end.

Something was wrong. This wasn't how a wolf would behave. As I looked more closely, I could see the fur seemed bushier and coarser than that of a wolf.

I edged slowly toward the animal. Huddled up against the building stood a black-eyed, shaggy-headed, dark-furred baby musk ox. I lowered my gun and stood there looking at this shy, frightened creature.

▼ Dogs resting during a whiteout. L to R: Roald, Robert, Lucy, Anna, and Douggie.

What a relief! Suddenly, I felt foolish. The poor musk ox had probably become separated in the fog from one of the herds grazing in the area. It looked healthy, so we quickly moved out, leaving it in peace.

Later that afternoon, we reached the Sagavanirktok River (locally known as "the Sag") and turned south toward our old camping spot near Catco in Prudhoe Bay. The dogs knew they were in familiar territory and picked up their pace. They raced down the river and made a hard right turn into Catco's parking lot. Suddenly they were speeding out of control.

They charged across the parking lot, leaped over a steep snowbank, slogged through several feet of deep snow, and abruptly halted at the exact place where they'd slept during our training. Without giving me a chance to unharness them, they began turning in circles, packing down the snow, and then curled up for a snooze.

I could hardly believe my eyes! In less than a minute, my gang of eight had gone from being a well-disciplined, orderly dog team to a tangled jumble of legs and lines. Yet looking down at their tired, furry bodies, I thought about how hard they'd worked and how contented they looked.

I dropped to my knees and began crawling alongside the team. One by one, I unsnapped and removed each harness, rolling the dog on its back to do so. I rubbed the dog's tummy, gave a big hug, and said, "Thank you for all your hard work." Not one dog looked at me. They all kept their eyes closed and bodies limp, in a state of total bliss, completely enjoying a few moments of love and heartfelt attention.

Soon I was enjoying my own bliss—a hot shower and full meal. The first leg of our journey was complete! As I ate and chatted with Prudhoe Bay friends, everyone had a good laugh over our encounter with a big, black, furry "wolf."

Good-bye, Prudhoe

The dogs rested for four days while I thawed an inch-thick crust of ice from the

---

Tent Defrosting

As I cooked and slept in my tent, water vapor from the cook stove and my own breath froze and stuck to the inside walls. Each morning I would kick the ice to break it into smaller pieces (which I threw out) so I could roll up my tent to leave camp. A small amount of ice would fall off, but most of it clung to the tent fibers and never melted in the freezing temperatures. By the end of a week or two on the trail, my tent was not only heavy with ice, but resembled a portable deepfreeze!

Whenever I came to a village, I asked permission to thaw my tent someplace where a sodden mass of meltwater would do no damage. Permission was usually granted to use the local fire hall. ☾

inside of my tent, inspected my equipment, and made repairs. Because there hadn't been much snow this year, broad stretches of gravel on the frozen rivers and on the tundra had badly damaged my sled runners. I installed new half-inch-thick, ultra-high-density plastic sled runners, tough enough to last the remaining 2,280 miles. Everything had to be in perfect working order, because from here on, villages would be few and far between. We would be on our own more than ever.

When I left Prudhoe Bay this time, I wouldn't be back. It was quite likely that I'd never again see the people I'd come to know there. A number of people had been friendly, helpful, and encouraging. I knew I would miss them. When I thought about that, it made me feel lonely.

At the same time, another part of my mind began taking over. I knew that, except for my dogs, I'd be spending lots of time alone in the next few months. I started shutting down socially, withdrawing from the people around me. I made no effort to talk to anyone. I think that's how my mind begins to deal with solitude. It's hard for people to understand, but it's what I have to do.

I focused entirely on preparing for the miles ahead. Again and again I went over each piece of equipment. I took only what was absolutely necessary, so I became compulsive about being sure every item was there. Any piece of gear, if lost, would be very difficult, perhaps impossible, to replace.

The last night in Prudhoe I splurged with long-distance phone calls to a few of my best friends. Everyone wished me luck, but only one friend, Dottie, told me she was confident we would make it. I always felt encouraged after talking to Dottie.

Somehow, although I was nervous and a little scared, I thought she was right.

After some brief good-byes, we left Prudhoe Bay for good on February 27. For the next few days, the weather was perfect.

FEBRUARY 28, 1993   -36°F   5 M.P.H. SE   35 MILES

The dogs are still looking happy and raring to go. We set out at a fast clip, heading east under a beautiful clear blue sky. It's a good feeling to watch the dogs moving along and enjoying themselves. The puppies aren't puppies anymore, now. They're over a year old and have developed into everything I could've hoped for. They're all hard-working, strong, healthy, and good-natured.

The only problem I have is with Roald. Whenever he starts out in the morning running beside his sister, Sojo, he always looks over at her and barks in her ear. He does it because he is so excited about starting out and he knows she'll let him get away with it.

▼ *Boundary marker at the edge of the Arctic National Wildlife Refuge.*

Sojo is sweetness personified. She will not stand up for herself against Roald. I've decided to embark on a campaign to build her confidence. Whenever we stop for a rest, I always walk up and pet everyone and talk a little to each dog. Usually I start with the front of the team and work back to the sled. Now, I've changed my pattern. I make a point of walking up to Sojo first and giving her attention. Then I start as usual at the front of the team and work back. This gives her twice as much attention as anyone else. Hopefully this will make her feel special and build her confidence.

When we reached Bullen that afternoon, I parked the team in the sun. The dogs could rest, but I had a big job ahead of me. The door to the room containing our cache was now almost completely buried behind a huge snowdrift.

After digging for about fifteen minutes, I finally managed to reach the door. The inside of the room was drifted halfway full, so I grabbed the edge of the door and started working it back and forth. Finally, the door would open far enough that, if I took off my parka, I could squeeze inside.

It was about -30°F, and the idea of standing around without my parka on was not very exciting. But I did it anyway. I shoveled and pushed and pulled as hard as I could to stay warm and get the door open. Finally, I got it open far enough to toss out the supplies and squeeze back outside, where I quickly donned my heavy, warm parka.

The dogs were bummed a bit by the increase in sled weight as we pulled out. They will have to get used to pulling a heavy load again. As we moved along, the wind changed from the SE to the NE and clouds starting coming in from the SW. All indications of a nasty storm.

We camped on the edge of the Arctic Ocean by the entrance to the Arctic National Wildlife Refuge (ANWR), after covering thirty-five miles. Considering all that happened today, that's a very respectable mileage.

As we left camp the next day, we sledded over to a tall, lonely-looking black pole on a small rise overlooking the tundra. It marked the boundary of the Arctic National Wildlife Refuge.

▲ *My camp beside an old abandoned trading post at Point Brownlow.*

We moved on to Point Brownlow and picked up the last cache from our training runs. Because we were making better time than I'd expected, we were getting ahead on supplies. That was better than being short on supplies, but tough on the dogs, who had to pull the extra weight. I noticed that the wind was blowing stronger and thought about setting up camp in the shelter of the buildings there. But it was only 2:00 P.M., too early to stop.

MARCH 1, 1993   -18°F   10–15 M.P.H. SW   20 MILES

As we left, I looked out over the Beaufort Sea and marveled at how different the ice looked from previous years. This stretch of ice had sometimes been a little rough, but usually there was enough flat ice to allow easy passage. This year the ice was pushed up in huge piles, well over twenty feet high. It was an awesome-looking sight. That nature has the power to hurl pieces of ice up like that, weighing thousands of pounds, is quite intimidating. Thank heavens there was a narrow stretch of beachfront that allowed us to pass through.

We'd only gone a little over seven miles when I realized I'd probably made a mistake. The storm I'd been watching for the last twenty-four hours was definitely coming and would overtake us soon. So, reluctantly, I stopped and pitched camp.

As I sit listening to the storm beating away at my tent wall, I really wish I'd stayed back at Point Brownlow.

MARCH 2, 1993   -20°F   10–15 M.P.H. SW   20 MILES

Amazingly, the storm died off during the night. But what a mess! Everything was drifted over. There was a small, snow-covered hump next to my tent, and I knew it hid my wonderful blue tarp. It took me two hours of digging to free up the tarp and remove the drifts from the back of the tent and dogsleds. But I didn't lose anything. The snow was so fine and powdery that it found its way into everything. Even the sled bag, which was lashed shut, was full of hard-packed snow. I finally got it cleaned out and repacked the sleds.

The dogs patiently watched me work and, as usual, started barking and jumping around when I brought out their harnesses. After they'd been harnessed, I lifted the hook and off we went.

As we slipped along over the hard-crusted snow, I watched my little gang of eight. Their furry ears turned backward to help keep the wind out. Their thick, bushy tails hung loosely, and their tough little padded feet moved lightly along. Even at twenty below, their coats kept them comfortably warm. Their tongues hung out just a tad to help them cool off. They were relaxed and happy, and watching them work was a beautiful sight.

By late afternoon we came to a camp of oil exploration workers. I headed straight for the kitchen and introduced myself. In the Arctic, it's considered rude to pass someone without stopping. Fortunately for me, it's also rude not to invite someone to stay for a meal!

Chicken, shrimp, peas, beans, potatoes, gravy, salad, and a table full of canned fruits and desserts—what a meal! As I ate, I visited with several of the workers.

They asked the usual questions and seemed genuinely enthusiastic about what I was doing. That was nice, because sometimes people will tell me they think I'm crazy, and they don't mean it as a compliment.

Blizzard Camping

I always set up my tent with the back toward the wind so that snow doesn't blow into my tent door when I open and close it. And I always put my gear outside in the same place, relative to the tent, so I'll know where to start digging after a storm.

My supplies are stored to the left of the tent under a big blue tarp. The bright blue tarp is easy to spot when I dig out and keeps snow from burying each individual item. The sleds sit about three feet away, runners to the wind, in front of the tent and tarp. The dogs are sheltered behind the sleds, out of the wind. This gives them maximum protection from the weather.

I always camp this way, even if the weather is clear. If a storm comes up in the night, I don't have to worry. I know everything is secure and nothing will be lost. ☾

Here, one man said he hoped he would have the chance someday to do something like I was doing. I hear this a lot and always try to explain my belief that anyone can do whatever he or she wants, if the person is willing to make the necessary sacrifices.

MARCH 4, 1993   -10°F   15 M.P.H. SW   38 MILES

We headed around the shoreline of Camden Bay. The ice in the middle of the bay was very rough, and I hoped to stay on the shoreline. But as we moved along, the beach began to narrow. Douggie stopped and looked back at me, waiting for me to tell him what to do.

I walked up on top of the bluff and looked around. There was very little snow cover on the tundra. Pulling the sleds over it would be terribly hard on the dogs. From my vantage point I could see out over the ice for miles. It looked broken and rough as far as I could see. But at least there was some snow on it. The sea was our best choice.

I told Douggie to go left. At first he just looked back at me, as though he was certain I'd made a mistake. He patiently waited for me to come to my senses. I called "Haw!" again, and he started left into the rubble ice. Then he turned back and started to climb up the bluff.

I couldn't really blame him. From his low eye level, the rubble ice must have looked impenetrable. So I set the hooks and walked ahead through the ice for about a hundred feet. Then I walked back, got on the sled, and called, "Douggie, haw!" He put his nose down, sniffed my tracks, and started moving along my trail. When he reached the point where I'd stopped, he stopped again and looked back at me.

Off the sled I got. I marched quickly through the ice for another hundred feet and then back to the sled. Over and over, we repeated the same procedure. Slowly, in hundred-foot increments, we moved forward.

After about three hours of struggle, we emerged next to Anderson Point at the east entrance to Camden Bay. As we drew closer, I saw a large pole sticking out of the ground atop a steep, ten-foot bluff.

I'd seen poles like that before in the Arctic. This one stood about twenty-five feet high, with steps cut into it almost all the way to the top, where a small platform rested. From there, people could have easily surveyed the land for game, or to see if hunters were returning. The lookout pole also served as a landmark. In a land that's almost totally flat, a tall, dark pole could be seen for miles to guide a returning hunter or traveler. In a storm, it might even save lives.

Beside the pole I found a drying rack made of thinner, shorter logs. Whoever once lived here would have hung caribou or polar bear hides to dry on this rack.

On the treeless tundra, where did this wood come from? The evidence was all around me. Every summer, trees float down the mighty Mackenzie River, more than two hundred miles east in Canada, to the Beaufort Sea. Ocean currents carry everything west along the northern coast of Alaska, though only a few trees make it this far west. Increasingly, as we moved east, the shore became cluttered with driftwood.

By six that evening we were in Kaktovik, a small Inuit village of about 250 people, located on Barter Island about seventy-five miles west of the Canadian border. It was the last village we would see in Alaska.

In spite of all the rough ice, we'd covered thirty-eight miles that day. I was enormously proud of the dogs. After taking care of them, I headed into the Waldo Arms Hotel for a shower. I'd contacted the hotel manager, Doug

Barrette, several weeks earlier to ask about finding someone to take out some supplies. Doug quickly fixed me up with a chicken dinner on the house and made arrangements to transport my provisions.

The next stretch, between Kaktovik and the first Canadian village, Tuktoyaktuk, was 320 miles. Because of the frequent storms this winter, I doubted we could carry enough supplies to make it that far. It was decided that the cache would be placed about seventy-five miles east near Demarcation Bay. I made the agreed-upon payment.

The dogs and I rested up a couple days, during which I washed laundry, picked up the dog food I'd previously mailed to the post office, and spoke to the kids in grades four to ten at the Harold Kaveolook school. I told them what I was doing, and why, and tried to encourage them to believe that they, too, could do something hard if they really put their minds to it. Everyone, I told them, has a right to try to make his or her dreams come true.

Good-bye, Alaska

MARCH 7, 1993   -14°F   5 M.P.H.   NE/SW   39 MILES

When we left this morning, we got into some rough ice on the Beaufort Sea right away, but I decided to run closer to shore and that helped a lot. There is a line of barrier islands along the coast here. As long as I stay inside them, the ice should be relatively smooth.

The dogs are slow but steady, even though the load is light. They've found their traveling pace and it looks like it's going to be slow. We spent a lot of time putting in caches during training and hauling heavy loads around. That made the dogs travel slowly, and once the pace is established for the season, it's very hard to change it. But we're doing well, and the dogs are happy and healthy, so I'm satisfied.

In the distance I can see the Brooks Range, which crosses much of the northern half of Alaska and comes almost down to the sea by the Alaska-Yukon border.

The border between the United States and Canada, marked so dramatically by the mountains, was less than forty miles away. Once we crossed that frontier, we would be sledding over land I'd never seen before. For weeks, during training, we'd been mushing back and forth across the North Slope of Alaska, often in areas I'd been to previously. The prospect of finally traveling over unknown terrain filled me with a new sense of exploration. When we camped that night, at the end of our first day out of Kaktovik, I stared off toward Canada feeling excited and happy, as if the expedition was now truly under way.

Then I noticed Roald was chewing on a tent stake and Matt had somehow managed to get hold of a food bowl and was trying to gnaw a hole in the bottom. It was time to feed the dogs.

MARCH 8, 1993 -2°F 20 M.P.H. SW 25 MILES

This morning it was whiteout and blowing snow. Visibility was very limited.

After breakfast I loaded up the sled and headed down the beach in search of the cache. I was feeling pretty nervous. The weather was nasty and visibility was deteriorating rapidly.

I wasn't certain exactly where our provisions had been cached, so I decided to sled along the beach where I could look out over the ice and across the tundra. This soon proved to be a mistake because the beach was clogged with driftwood. Dogs know what trees are for and so we kept stopping every few inches. I yelled at them to keep moving but no sooner did they advance than a sled would get stuck.

While I struggled to free the sled, the dogs discovered more trees. After about half an hour of this I was beside myself with frustration. To make matters worse, the dog lines kept getting snagged on upraised roots and branches and soon the dogs were bunched in a tight little knot. Robert didn't like having all the other dogs beside him, Matt kept trying to get acquainted with Sojo, Roald kept trying to straighten out Matt, and Lucy and Alice quit working altogether. Anna was wagging her tail and thoroughly enjoying all the excitement. Everyone was totally oblivious to my rantings. Poor Douggie stood looking stoically out over the tundra with a detached expression on his face that clearly asked, Why me?

Sometime later I found the cache at a spot where three cabins stood. I'd been there once before, on a trip I'd taken in 1986. I remembered thinking then that this was the most beautiful place on Earth. I wanted to camp here and soak up some more of that beauty. If only the weather would improve!

For once the weather favored me. The next day was perfect.

MARCH 9, 1993   0°F   LIGHT WINDS, NEARLY CLEAR SKY   0 MILES

What a wonderful gift nature gave us when it created this part of the world! To the people who once lived off the land, this must have been paradise. To the west are seemingly endless miles of open tundra that would have sustained abundant caribou and musk ox. To the south and southeast stand the magnificent mountains of the Brooks Range, with their jagged, snow-covered peaks. These mountains would have provided berries, greens, and small land mammals.

To the east is Demarcation Bay, providing fish and a large, protected harbor. Beyond lies the Arctic Ocean with its char, whitefish, seals, whales, and polar bears. The beach is strewn with hundreds of logs to provide building material and firewood.

To a people who lived off the land, this was all anyone could have asked for. Food, shelter, and beauty. With the exception of a few passing hunters or summer adventurers, no one ever comes here anymore. It's like a land stuck in time. The air is so pure it has no smell. The land is so silent it has no sound.

Subsistence Living

Subsistence living means obtaining enough food and clothing directly from the environment to maintain life. Native people in the Arctic have hunted and fished for their subsistence for centuries, surviving in one of the harshest environments on Earth.

Caribou and salmon continue to be the main food sources for many people living in the Arctic today. Subsistence hunting and fishing is a necessity because of the high cost of commodities in these isolated communities so far from commercial centers. Most Arctic villages lack roads to the outside world, so everything must be flown in at great expense. At the same time, few wage-paying jobs are available.

Every year, during the annual caribou migrations across the Arctic, people hunt the animals to feed their families. The meat is often preserved in cellars dug deep into the frozen earth. Each summer, men, women, and children catch salmon and other fish to supply food for themselves, as well as for their dogs. The fish are either frozen or dried on racks. As they have done for centuries, people still travel to fish camps and hunting camps, places where the fishing or hunting is especially good.

Wild berries are also an important source of food in the Arctic. Picked by the gallons in the summer, they are preserved in animal oils or by freezing. ☾

▼ *Viewing grave markers near Demarcation Bay in Alaska.*

This area, so rich with resources for subsistence living, was as beautiful as I remembered. I spent the day exploring the area, imagining what life might have been like for the Native peoples and non-Native traders who once lived here. I found many of their abandoned log cabins and sod huts, as well as some old wooden grave markers. I stared at the inscriptions on the rough planks, trying to make out the names and dates: Annie, 1913, and Alonik, 1922.

It was impossible not to feel the history of the place. Who were Annie and Alonik? Were they young, or old, when they died? What was the story of their lives? I would never know, but I wished I could.

We easily covered the five miles across Demarcation Bay the following day, despite fully loaded sleds, now heavy with fresh provisions. On the other side, we stopped to investigate an abandoned whaling ship that must have been beached decades ago. A huge snowdrift reached almost up to the deck, so I was able to climb right on board.

Whaling in the Arctic

Commercial whaling is no longer permitted under the rules of the International Whaling Commission (IWC). This is a voluntary agreement that most countries abide by. Native peoples in Alaska, however, are still allowed to hunt whales as part of their subsistence lifestyle. The Native people work closely with the IWC to ensure that not too many whales are taken. They are anxious to protect the whale species, after witnessing the near-elimination of the bowhead whale by commercial hunters earlier in this century.

Whaling has always been a tremendously important part of Native culture in the Arctic. In 1988 the people of Barrow renewed the celebration called *Kivgiq*. Now, every other spring, Inupiat people from all over Alaska come together after the whale harvest to feast, play games, and celebrate their bounty and good fortune. In the spring of 1993, while I was on the expedition, Native people from Russia and Canada came to join in the festival for the first time. ☽

MARCH 10, 1993   -10°F   10 M.P.H. NE/SW   25 MILES

On its deck stood huge, six-feet-wide and three-feet-deep pots that rested on steel stands about eight feet in the air. These must have been used to render the whale oil out of the blubber and placed high in the air to help keep the stench out of the sailors' faces.

The ship looked to be about a hundred and fifty feet long and was in excellent shape. I went below deck but found only empty rooms that appeared to serve as cargo holds, crew quarters, and galley.

The abandoned whaler was beached a few miles west of the Canadian border. As I stood in that beautiful place, I hoped that no type of tourism would ever be permitted there. No matter how carefully planned and executed, even eco-tourism would change the land forever. I wanted—and still want—some places on Earth to be left alone. We almost took all the bowhead whales. I hope we are smart enough not to take all the land.

Leaving the ship, I lifted the snowhooks and sledded over toward the Canadian border. After a little searching, I found a three-foot-high obelisk standing a few feet back from the shore. This was all that marked the boundary between the United States and Canada. It was covered with dozens of initials scratched in the white paint, so I carved "PF" on the American side. Then we slipped over an imaginary line into Canada. ☽

THE EXPEDITION: ACROSS CANADA

IV

❂

Old Dog

MARCH 11, 1993   -5°F   20 M.P.H. SW   28 MILES

Today was absolutely terrible. Punchy snow forced us off the tundra and down onto the sea ice. The sled got stuck about two million times, flipped over at least one million times, and I had to retie the load onto the trailer sled no fewer than half a million times. It took four-and-a-half hours to cover just thirteen miles.

We finally found some smooth ice closer in to shore. About that time I saw the first Canadian DEW Line site called Bar 1. It was still active, so I decided to go over for a little rest and maybe some lunch.

As we pulled up behind the main building, two Eskimo dogs came charging over a high snowdrift and started barking furiously and running around my team.

I thought someone would come out to take control of their dogs, but after several minutes no one appeared. I took this to mean that this DEW Line station did not welcome visitors, and left.

The two dogs were large and furry. One was a male and was light reddish brown; the other was a white female. They escorted us as we moved along, always keeping a steady distance of about a hundred yards. They were quite a distraction to my team, but Douggie once again kept everyone in line.

We were about thirteen miles past the DEW Line site when the storm that had been chasing us all day finally started to catch up. The male dog was nowhere to be seen, but the female was slinking around as I set up camp.

I fed the dogs and looked around over the tundra. No sign of either dog. The Eskimo dogs were probably already back home.

The next morning I woke up to whiteout—and the white dog! She'd sneaked into camp sometime during the night and fallen asleep beside the tent. I began packing up, but she just ignored me and continued sleeping. Finally, when I pulled the tent apron out from under her, she moved.

The last thing I needed was an extra dog to distract the team and eat their rations. I came up with a plan to get rid of her. Just as we were about to leave, I set out a large pile of food for her. By the time she finished it, we'd be long gone and she would go home.

My plan seemed to work. We sledded over the tundra along lagoons and bays toward Herschel Island. The small, rolling hills were covered in six inches of soft snow—very deep for unpacked snow in the Arctic. We passed several tumbledown cabins and, once, almost drove right over the top of an old sod hut. Posts formerly used as drying racks stuck up out of the ground.

It was getting to feel like spring now. Temperatures were approaching zero and fairly consistent. I noticed some bluffs along the coast with deep piles of snow on their sides—perfect sites for polar bear dens. Mother bears and their cubs would soon be emerging from their dens, so we stayed well off shore. Several times, when the dogs seemed to smell something and then speed up for no apparent reason, I suspected we were probably passing polar bear dens.

A little after noon we stopped for lunch. The dogs were resting, and I was lazing on the sled, enjoying a cup of tea. Suddenly Matt jumped up and began barking. It was a bark that meant "animal approaching."

I immediately thought *polar bear.*

And indeed, when I leapt off the sled and spun around to look, a white, furry animal was walking toward me. But it wasn't a bear. It was that pesky white Eskimo dog!

I ran toward her, flailing my arms and yelling at her to go home. She just rolled over on her side. I tried to make her get up, but she wouldn't budge. When she finally got up, I tried to shove her toward home, but she rolled over onto the ground again.

No matter what I did, I could not get rid of that dog! When we took off, she slowly padded along behind us.

By early afternoon another storm was closing in, so I stopped to set up camp. Just as I finished, the white dog came waddling up. I thought she looked like a very old dog, so I named her Old Dog.

As pitiful as she looked, I hardened my heart. Her presence disrupted the team. When I fed the dogs that night, I did not feed her. Tomorrow, I hoped, she would take her empty stomach and go home.

MARCH 13, 1993   -2°F   25 M.P.H. W/NW, GUSTING TO 40 M.P.H.
0 MILES, STORM

Storm and no travel. I finally felt obligated to feed Old Dog since she can't be expected to walk home in this weather.

What else could I do? I was stuck. I couldn't let her starve, even if she was uninvited. Grudgingly, I shared the team's hard-earned food with Old Dog, knowing she'd never go home once I did. Still, I vowed not to let myself get attached to her.

MARCH 14, 1993   -2 F°   25 M.P.H. W/NW   0 MILES, STORM

More storm. No travel. I gave all the dogs a pedicure, excluding Old Dog, of course. They need their nails clipped occasionally, just like people. If they get too long, the nails will force the toes up as the dogs run and can cause split nails, which are painful.

The decision to travel when it's windy is based on whether I think I can get the tent up. If I think I can raise it in the wind, we travel. If not, we don't move. Today, I don't think I can get the tent up, so we wait.

The weather improved the next day, so we broke camp, heading toward the Babbage River and on to King Point. Old Dog followed, but at a respectful distance, probably because I made a point of glaring at her whenever she got too close to the team.

MARCH 15, 1993   -16°F   35 M.P.H. SE   36 MILES

Amazingly, Old Dog has managed to keep up. She travels about a quarter-mile behind us and drops down to rest every time we stop. Occasionally she tries to come up to the team, but I don't like that, so she generally stays back.

Incredible though it may seem, another big storm was coming.

I headed into the wind, toward some steep bluffs to the south to find shelter. It was so hard to make progress that I got off the sled and led the dogs. I could lean about thirty degrees into the wind and still not fall over. I felt like I might be lifted into the air at any moment.

Farther on, the cliffs provided more protection. We traveled back out onto the sea ice. Although smooth enough for sledding, it was glare ice—slick, smooth, and polished to a shine. The wind pushed the sled like a sail, several times knocking it sideways, out of control.

The sled picked up so much speed that once, when it hit a little chunk of ice, it flew into the air and landed upside down, pinning my left arm under the sled bag. It was fairly easy to get my arm out and right the sled, but the incident really scared the dogs. They huddled together, looking at me with frightened faces. An out-of-control sled always frightens a dog team. They fear being run over. But I wanted them to understand that it really wasn't a danger and that they must deal with unexpected problems. So I lined them out right away, reassured them, and insisted that we keep going.

The next day we reached King Point, a place I'd read about and looked forward to visiting for many years. Here the Norwegian explorer Roald Amundsen and his crew of six men spent the winter of 1905, along with the crew of a whaling ship that had gone aground.

Amundsen and his men were sailing a little ship called the *Gjoa* through the Northwest Passage from east to west. They began in 1903 and finished in 1906, accomplishing for the first time in recorded history a journey that numerous other explorers had attempted.

When they arrived at King Point in the fall of 1905, it was too late in the year to sail around Alaska and home to Norway. So they stayed the winter. While there, they continued measuring the Arctic's magnetic field, a task they'd undertaken throughout their journey. Their measurements answered one of the major scientific questions of the day, determining that the Magnetic North Pole does not stay in one place, but moves around.

King Point had been a major whaling center for more than a century. Remains of many cabins were still standing. I decided to take the rest of the day off to look around.

MARCH 16, 1993 -10°F 25–45 M.P.H. SW 23 MILES

To me, Amundsen was the ultimate hero. He was a meticulous planner. He took excellent care of his men. He was smart enough to adapt to the Inuit ways, and wore their clothes and learned to travel by dog team. He was cautious almost to a fault, but he succeeded where so many others had failed. He simply took the time to prepare properly, and he knew what he was doing. To realize that I was probably walking where Amundsen had walked was an enormous thrill and worth everything it had taken to get this far.

The King Point area had many cabins around it. Douggie showed himself to be an outstanding leader and followed intricate commands as we toured the sights. I love that dog, and I love my entire gang of eight.

I'm even starting to develop a little affection for Old Dog.

▼ *Molly the DEW Line dog walking past an old cabin at King Point, a place where Anarulunguaq spent time and where my hero Roald Amundsen spent an entire winter.*

I couldn't help it. Old Dog was so determined, I had to admire her persistence and spirit of adventure.

The next day at Shingle Point, another DEW Line station, I learned that Old Dog was actually called Molly. Furthermore, Molly was something of an explorer in her own right. She'd made a career of traveling back and forth along the arctic coast.

MARCH 17, 1993 0°F 15 M.P.H. SW/SE 27 MILES

Molly would do what she'd done with me, which was to follow anyone who came along, and refuse to go home. Eventually, whoever she was following would have to give in and start feeding her.

She'd followed us for about 75 miles. But her biggest adventure had come a few years back. She'd taken up with a group of hunters heading east and followed them almost 250 miles to Tuktoyaktuk, where she took up with another group of hunters heading west and followed them all the way back home to Bar 1.

Molly, it turned out, was a famous dog. Her exploits were known throughout the DEW Line system.

Workers at Shingle Point assured me they would take care of Molly until she could be flown home to Bar 1 on the next supply plane.

The last time I saw Old Molly, she was waddling into a building, happily following a bowl full of meat scraps from the cook. Now that's the life for a dog!

Mackenzie Maze

After leaving Shingle Point, we entered the Mackenzie River Delta, a maze of frozen river channels lined with steep banks and willow thickets. The stubby, two-foot shrubs were the closest thing to trees we'd seen in more than three months—a welcome sight until we tried moving through them. My idea that it would be quickest to head straight across the delta was quickly proven wrong.

MARCH 18, 1993   -4°F   15 M.P.H. S/SE   32 MILES

Douggie remembered the hard struggle yesterday and didn't want to enter the thicket. I couldn't blame him. We took an early lunch break and I climbed a nearby pingo to look around. I could see no way around this jungle that lay ahead of us.

I gave Douggie the command to go forward and he reluctantly pushed his head into the first bunch of branches. The snow was punchy and about a foot deep. The willow branches kept grabbing at the gangline and, in the course of an hour, managed to snag Lucy, Sojo, Roald, Robert, Matt, Anna, Alice, and Douggie. Every time a dog got snagged, our little train came to a stop and I had to wade up and free their line. Even more frustrating was when the sled ran into the base of a willow tree and got jammed. I had to dig the snow out from around the sled runners and pull it sideward to get it free.

The dogs were hot and frustrated, and so was I, when we finally came to a narrow channel just after midday. I got out my map and studied it carefully. If we followed this channel north, it would take us to another channel, which would take us to another channel, and so on, all the way across the twenty-five-mile-wide delta.

Had I understood the density of the vegetation and the enormous size of the delta, I would have avoided it altogether. Now the next-best choice was to avoid the brush by following the frozen channels. The labyrinth of channels would mean many more miles, but much less frustration.

Before we continued, I changed leaders. Anna had been leading with Douggie for several hours, and doing well, but I didn't want to stress her. I moved Alice, her mother, up front for a while.

As we were sledding down a side channel, every time Alice saw a leaf blowing along the ice toward her, she would try to grab it as it blew by. It was rather poor form for a lead dog, but she was having fun and working at the same time, so I let it go. Thank heavens I have these dogs with me! No matter how tired I am or how hard the day has been, they always seem to do something to make me laugh.

Sometimes during the day I look at my face in the mirror on my compass to check for frostbite. The eyes I see looking back at me look very tired lately.

I was tired, and I knew it, but I couldn't relax. Already we'd lost so many travel days to stormy weather that I was constantly concerned about running out of food and supplies. Rather than rest, I pushed on.

MARCH 19, 1993   -2°F   15 M.P.H. W   33 MILES

Anna was apparently watching her mother yesterday and has taken up the hobby of leaf chasing. She was a little less disciplined about it than her mother, running all over and not working enough. So I put her back in the team and moved Robert up.

Douggie and Robert led us through the last of several channels, through a land that grew steadily hillier. Suddenly we broke out of the hills. Ahead of us was the main channel of the Mackenzie River and the ice road.

Every year the government plows the snow off the Mackenzie River to create an ice road from Inuvik all the way to Tuktoyaktuk. Normally "Tuk" is not connected to the rest of the world by road.

It was almost glare ice, but after a while we reached a better snow-packed section and were moving along just fine when a large snowplow came up behind us. I told Douggie to "gee" off the road. Without missing a step, he promptly led us over a high snowbank and onto the tundra.

I was really proud of him. For a dog to leave a nice trail, climb a snow-bank, and go out onto the tundra where there is no trail, is very good.

Our arrival in Tuktoyaktuk the morning of March 21 created quite a canine uproar. Every dog in the village began barking at the same moment. Hoping to quiet things down, I set up camp on the outskirts of town, then headed for the nearest hot shower and meal.

Tuktoyaktuk is one of the biggest Native villages in the Arctic. I guessed the population to be about 1,200. Wooden houses built very close together lined the streets, which were overhung with utility wires. Most people walked or drove snowmobiles around the town.

At the Tuk Inn, cook, waitress, and dishwasher Doreen Church handed me a stack of towels and *two* bars of soap. I guess she figured I needed a little extra scrubbing! Once I was clean and fit for humans, she brought out a full-course dinner: soup, barbecued ribs, corn, potatoes and gravy, and glass after glass of good, fresh water. I ate it all, relishing every bite, then finished with cherry pie and fresh coffee. Afterward, I couldn't move. I sat in the warm dining room in a digestive stupor, thinking life was pretty good.

The next day I visited the local school to pick up my supplies. The previous fall, in preparation for the trip, I'd contacted the school principal in each community along my route, beginning with Tuktoyaktuk, and asked if they would hold my supplies for me. In return, I'd promised to talk to students in the school. Every principal had agreed, so I'd mailed dry dog food, rice, nuts, dried fruits, candy, tea, and cocoa to all the schools along the way. At this school I helped judge the students' science fair.

That evening I was invited to dinner at the home of Eddie Gruben and his family. Eddie entertained us for hours with stories about his life as a young man. He claimed to be the first Inuit to own a snowmobile, and perhaps he was. Today, he owns a large transportation company that supplies fuel and other commodities in trucks specially adapted for crossing the tundra. I was glad for the chance to laugh and visit with this kind, welcoming family.

Everyone in this town was friendly to me, even bringing gifts of frozen fish for the dogs and fresh fruit and meat for me; it was tempting to stay longer. But I decided we'd better move on while the weather was good. The next village, Paulatuk, lay about 300 miles away, so I had to pack a heavy load of supplies to get us through.

The next day, as I was preparing to leave, a steady stream of visitors came by. I'll never forget four students from the College of the Arctic. After we'd talked a while, one of them said, "Well, if you croak, at least people will write about you that you did what you wanted."

I told him that was one of the nicest things anyone had ever said about me!

Dogs on Strike

MARCH 24, 1993   +8°F   15 M.P.H.   23 MILES

We traveled slowly today. The fog made it hard for me to see, and the heavy load made it hard for the dogs to pull the sleds.

It's always a trade-off where supplies are concerned. Do you travel slowly with lots of supplies so you can sit out a storm or two? Or do you travel light and fast and hope that everything goes well? Experience has taught me that it's better to be safe than sorry out here. After all, there isn't a local corner store to run down to if we get caught short.

Clearly, the dogs were unhappy about the heavy sled loads. I was feeling pretty lousy, too, having picked up another dose of cold germs in Tuk. But in my typical fashion, I was determined to push on. Most of the weight came from food, so I figured morale would improve in a few days as we ate up our rations and my cold got better.

As it turned out, I was wrong.

MARCH 28, 1993   -24°F   20 M.P.H. SE   21 MILES

Robert and Anna ran lead today for a while so Douggie could have a break. Robert did okay, but Anna did even better. She's emerging as a new lead dog.

For some reason, around noon the dogs began to really mess up. If I called "gee," they wouldn't make a slight turn to the right; instead, they'd make a sharp 90-degree turn. If I called "haw" to try to correct them back on course, they would turn 180 degrees and head straight left. After a couple hours of this, I was frustrated and angry.

The more they screwed up, the madder I got. The madder I got, the more they screwed up. By midafternoon, we'd come 19.4 "crow" miles. The wind was picking up speed and the dogs kept looking toward the south. I knew they were hearing the sound of the storm rushing across the ice toward us. A sudden gust hit us broadside, stinging our faces with blowing snow.

The dogs had had enough and went on strike. They just simply stopped pulling and curled up for a nap.

I saw flaming red and jammed the hook into the snow. My first thought was to storm up there and yank every one of them up by the scruffs of their furry necks. But before I was even past the sled, I knew it would be pointless. They were tired, bummed out, and a storm was coming.

When a team goes on strike, it's time for the driver to take a cold, hard look in the mirror.

I set up camp, thinking about what had happened. The situation was not good. We weren't making much progress. And no one was having fun anymore.

In the last two weeks, we'd come through some rough terrain. The dogs had worked hard, with only one-and-a-half days off. I'd had even fewer. I realized it had been a mistake not to rest longer in Tuk. Trying to haul the heavy load ourselves, in an attempt to save money, was also a mistake. Though my funds were dwindling rapidly, in this case it would have been wiser to hire someone in Tuk to haul out a cache for us.

I decided not to travel the next day, no matter how good the weather. I promised myself that when we reached Paulatuk, we would rest for three full days.

I spent most of that next day melting water and feeding the dogs while they lazed around in the sunshine. I fed them all until they wouldn't eat another bite and, as usual, gave Sojo a little extra attention. They seemed to appreciate the break, and I hoped we'd made a big enough dent in the dog food to lighten the sled load.

MARCH 30, 1993   -15°F   5 M.P.H. SE   39 MILES

The dogs practically flew out of camp this morning. By 1:00 P.M. we'd already come nineteen miles! The dogs are happy and spirited and energetic. It was well worth taking a day off.

I feel so much better myself now. Not so grouchy. I think the dogs and I sense each other's moods. When there is a problem, it affects all of us.

When we reached the entrance to Harrowby Bay, a ptarmigan was flying along the beach, and the dogs started chasing it. It kept flying just in front of us, going our way, so I let the dogs run. They were enjoying it, and there was no way they could possibly catch or hurt the bird.

I stopped the team after a bit, but the ptarmigan landed just a few feet away and kept calling. The noise excited the dogs and off we went again. We stopped, and the bird stopped. The bird called, and we chased after it. The bird actually seemed to be enjoying this little game. After all, there isn't much excitement around here. A ptarmigan has to take whatever it can get!

The terrain began to change markedly. We soon entered a riverbed about one-quarter mile wide that wound through soft, white, snow-covered hills. There were many canyons among these hills, and I had to pay close attention so that we didn't get off the main river channel.

South of here lie the Smoking Hills. Centuries ago, underground coal deposits spontaneously ignited and began smoldering under the surface. The result is vapor rising from the hills, which gives them the appearance of smoking. The burning coal sends the bitter odor of sulfur into the air. It can be smelled for miles. I hope this doesn't keep up too long. It sure is stinky.

Runaway Dogs

MARCH 31, 1993   -12°F   LIGHT SW WIND   30 MILES

A very frightening thing happened about 2:00 P.M. today. We were sledding toward the top of the pass when Robert suddenly started looking off about forty-five degrees toward the right. I could see something over where he was looking, but my glasses had fogged up and were now in my pocket. All the dogs were barking excitedly while I got the glasses out and put them on.

I saw it was a pair of arctic foxes. Just then, Alice, who was running behind in the swing position, bit the towline through in her excitement and set the four front-end dogs free. Douggie, Robert, Lucy, and Anna suddenly went tearing off across the tundra in hot pursuit of the foxes.

I tried calling them back, but I don't think they even heard me. The foxes headed for the hills, followed by my four dogs, followed by the remaining four dogs and me.

When we reached the base of the steep hills, I secured my shrunken team and started trying to track the other four dogs, who were already out of sight. At first their tracks were easy to see. But as I got higher, the snow became harder and their tracks were less obvious. Finally, I reached a long stretch of rock-hard snow, on a small divide between two hills, where the tracks seemed to just disappear.

As I looked over the divide, my heart sank. They could have gone in any number of directions. I stood there calling, listening, hoping, but there was no response, just the sound of the wind. I felt frightened, because I knew there were wolves back in the hills. If they saw my dogs, the wolves would kill them.

I walked back to where I'd last seen a track and started searching again. Only this time I bent down and looked very carefully at the snow. When I found the exact spot where the tracks disappeared, I made a small depression in the snow with the heel of my boot and started looking carefully to the left and then to the right, just two feet at a time. Then I moved forward and repeated the process.

Suddenly I saw just the tiniest scratch in the snow off to my right. That was it! The dogs had gone to the right and over the divide. I went charging down the side of the hill into the valley, following their trail. As I came down the valley, the sled and dogs came into view and I saw the best sight in the world. There were two sets of four dogs each! My runaway dogs had come back on their own.

When I finally came huffing and puffing up to them, my fear and worry melted into joy. I was so happy to see them that I hugged each one.

Polar Bear Scare

The next day, as we continued toward Paulatuk, I was hoping for a stretch of quiet, uneventful dog mushing. As the day wore on, I seemed to be getting my wish.

About four in the afternoon we left the Horton River and broke through the hills onto Franklin Bay, dropping onto a flat, frozen beach with just a scant covering of snow. The sky was clear and blue, and as we rounded a curve, the sun shone warm on my face. At last, I thought, Douggie and I could relax.

We headed south along the Smoking Hills, with about ninety miles remaining to Paulatuk. Above us, on the right, stood some bluffs with snow-filled ravines and high snowdrifts. To reward Douggie for his hard work through the mountains, I gave him a break from leading. The terrain was so easy that I put Robert in lead, figuring even he could manage to run straight down the beach. Then I leaned against the handlebar to enjoy a nice, gentle ride.

Shortly thereafter, trouble began.

APRIL 1, 1993   -2°F   5 M.P.H. NW   30 MILES

As we came around a slight corner, I saw a polar bear about a hundred yards away, standing up in a ravine, nursing her cub. She looked so beautiful. She didn't move, just stood there watching us as we went by.

Because the bears were above eye level, I was praying that we would get by them without any of the dogs seeing them. But just as we came even with them, Robert looked over and saw them. Robert is very social and decided to go visiting.

At first the other dogs didn't see them. I told Douggie to "haw" to help keep us going straight. Then, suddenly, everyone saw them.

Douggie tried to obey my demands that we go left, but he couldn't overcome the power of the seven other dogs. Almost instantly we were racing toward the bears at breakneck speed. I stood on the brake with both feet, but the scant snow on the frozen beach provided no place for the brake to bite. With my feet still on the brake, I grabbed a snowhook and bent over to try to jam it into the beach. It just skidded uselessly along. With all my might, I tried to create enough drag to at least slow us down, but nothing had any effect.

When we reached the bottom of the snow-filled ravine, the brake and hook suddenly dug in hard. Everything was jerked to a jarring halt. By then Robert and Douggie were standing only about three feet from the bear, who was slowly backing up. She'd gotten her little cub behind her and kept looking back at it.

She was small, as polar bears go, only about six feet long and three feet tall at the shoulder. Her coat was the pure white of a young bear. Even so, I knew better than to underestimate her strength. A polar bear can snag a full-grown seal from its den beneath the ice with one scoop of its deadly, white paw.

The dogs were barking wildly and lunging toward her. Finally, she made a false charge at the dogs. She ran at them with her mouth open and hit Douggie in the head, sending him sprawling down the slope. She seemed to have hit him almost by accident. When the team fell back, she turned around and scurried back to her cub.

I grabbed hold of the gangline and screamed, "No! No! Stop! Douglas, stop!" But it was useless. The gangline jerked out of my hands, sending me sprawling.

The dogs charged the bear. Again, the bear made a false charge toward the dogs. Back and forth they went at least five times. Finally, the bear started to get angry. She wagged her head back and forth and started to hiss.

I retreated to the back of the sled and pulled out my shotgun. Until now she'd been demonstrating only defensive behavior. She was starting to become aggressive. The last thing I wanted to do was shoot a mother bear with a cub. But I couldn't let her kill one of my dogs.

Suddenly she made a false charge—and kept coming. Almost instantly, she was in the middle of the team, lunging left and right as the panicked dogs kept yapping.

Then, to my total amazement, everything suddenly stopped! The adversaries stood silently looking at each other.

I decided this might be the only chance I had to distract everyone. I was very uncertain about whether or not I was doing the right thing. I moved forward and held out my hand, palm forward. "It's okay. It's okay," I said. "We're going now."

The bear then moved her head in my direction. Her coal-black eyes met mine. She seemed to be seeing me for the first time.

For a terrifying instant, I thought I'd made a deadly mistake. Then she just turned to go back. She started to walk toward the opening of her den, which was a small hole on top of the high snowdrift to our right. The cub followed closely behind.

By now I'd moved past the front of the sled and turned the team around. We were moving forward when the sled hit something under the snow and came to a sudden stop.

It was in that instant that she must have stopped to turn around and look at us. She stepped forward, as if to tell us not to try anything. The dogs apparently saw this as an aggressive move and spun around to try to meet her attack. As the sled whipped around, I was knocked off my feet, and my right leg got caught in the gangline.

Suddenly I was on my back in front of the sled runners, being dragged helplessly up the ravine. It seemed to me that we were rocketing up the slope.

I could do nothing to stop what was happening. The thought went through my mind that I was probably going to die very soon. In a rather detached way, I wondered if it was going to hurt and what would happen to any of the surviving dogs.

Suddenly one of the snowhooks bit. The sled jerked to a halt. I looked frantically around for the bear, but she was nowhere in sight. She had hightailed it into her den.

As I extracted myself from the lines, only her little cub remained outside the opening. While I tried to get everything turned around, the cub stood there for almost a minute, bravely hissing at us, and then silently slipped inside to the warmth and safety of its mother.

This time, as we headed at full speed toward the frozen beach, nothing stopped us. As quickly as possible, I wanted to put miles between us and those bears.

Everything had happened so quickly that I hadn't had time to feel much fear. Now that it was over, my whole body began to shake. As we scooted along the beach, my legs suddenly gave out. I couldn't even stand on the runners, but had to cling to the handlebar for support.

After a few moments I understood what was happening. The after-effects of adrenaline were setting in. Though I hadn't realized it at the time, adrenaline had been surging through my body during the encounter. Now my body was ridding itself of all the excess energy by shaking.

I longed to camp and rest, but didn't dare until we'd covered more miles. Gradually strength returned to my legs and I was able to stand. As we sledded along, I could feel myself calming down. My body was returning to normal.

After a while, we rounded a slight corner. There stood a giant, thirty-foot grizzly bear on its hind legs, ready to pounce!

Instantly I was terrified all over again. My heart pounded as more adrenaline shot through my veins. Then I realized that the "grizzly" was nothing more than an outcropping of brown rock. My mind was still racing in overdrive, enough to play tricks on me.

Farther along, a polar bear appeared off to my right. It looked so real that I yelled at Douggie to "haw." Then I saw it was just a large, snow-covered rock.

Similar bear mirages popped up again and again. I began to get angry with myself. After all, what if a real problem came up? I had to get hold of myself and separate reality from hallucination.

By evening we'd traveled about five miles down the beach from the bears. I set up camp out on the sea ice, away from land. When I checked Douggie's face I found a one-inch wound where the mother bear had punctured his cheek. I didn't stitch it, but gave him some antibiotics to prevent infection.

That night, as I wrote the details of the day in my journal, my hands still shook.

Sad and Cold

Thankfully, the rest of the trip to Paulatuk was uneventful. I kept my promise and rested there for three days. During that time, I called my veterinarian back home to ask about Douggie's wound, which worried me. Both the vet and the nurse at the Paulatuk health clinic reassured me that it was healing fine.

I also called a friend and received news that broke my heart. Dottie Nicholson, one of the friends I'd called from Barrow before starting the trip, had died of a heart attack. I was stunned and overcome with sadness. Dottie had been such a good friend, always encouraging me on expeditions. It was a small comfort to recall our last long and good conversation. More than ever, I wanted to fulfill her faith in me by completing this journey.

In Paulatuk I learned one more thing: I wasn't imagining that the winter was unusually stormy. The school principal told me that normally they closed school only two days a year due to bad weather. Already this year they'd closed for sixteen days—the same number of days I'd been stormbound.

Before we left Paulatuk, I arranged to have a cache taken out about eighty miles to the east side of Albert Bay. On April 8 we sledded out of town in a thick ice fog. I figured we'd reach the cache in two days and then continue to the next village, Coppermine. By the end of the day the fog cleared, but the next day bitter winds from the north began to plague us, forcing even Douggie to stop and hunker down. The third day we managed only five miles. I set up camp with hands so numb from cold that they could barely grasp the tent, which blew down repeatedly as I tried to stake it.

The landscape was beautiful, all the snow polished to a satin sheen by the constant wind. But most of the time my hands stung so badly I couldn't enjoy the view. By the fourth day, we were almost completely out of food. We had to reach our cache that day, or sit out an oncoming storm without fuel or food. I was feeling pretty anxious. The wind was so cold that Anna and Douggie were the only dogs willing to run lead and take on the full brunt of the wind.

Fortunately we reached the cache on April 11, and just in time. For four days straight we couldn't travel.

APRIL 13, 1993   -5°F   20–45 M.P.H. NE   0 MILES, STORM

Everything was whiteout. Chaos. Fed the dogs and shoveled them out and stood up to listen. I could hear the sea ice grinding and breaking even above the noise of the storm. This wind seems to go on forever. It's easy to lose perspective. It's depressing to lose so much travel time. This is a huge, powerful storm. I just wish it would stop.

APRIL 14, 1993   20–40 M.P.H. E   0 MILES, STORM

I got out of the tent and walked into the wind with my heavy clothing on. It's almost impossible to walk. I have to lean into it, and the gusts almost knock me down.

APRIL 16, 1993   +2°F   20 M.P.H. E

Packed up this morning in fairly strong wind. The pass into Amundsen Gulf was horrible—strong wind and blowing snow. I was pretty lost most of the time, but I could see the dim outline of hills on either side of us, so I kept going up a little valley. When we got down to the sea ice it continued to blow worse than I expected. Slowly it got better.

All colors are vivid today. Tomorrow will be better. I was feeling pretty intimidated these last few days. I have some confidence back today. I hope Douggie gets some back, also. The wind has been hard on him, especially, because he has to look into it to see where he's going.

APRIL 17, 1993   0°F   10 M.P.H. E / 20 M.P.H. S   35 MILES

Got off to a nice start this morning with moderate headwind. The dogs don't seem to mind. Anna ran lead with Douggie all day, which gives us some speed. But she stops to investigate things a lot. Still a puppy in some ways.

Anna follows the command "gee" very well now. Funny how dogs learn "gee" before "haw."

Sojo Barks Back

In this stretch of Amundsen Gulf we came across two vessels abandoned on the beach. One, a lifeboat, had a huge hole near the bow. The other was a rusting Hudson's Bay Company ship called the *Nechilik*, which was built in 1942 and ran aground in 1957. The dogs took a break while I climbed aboard to investigate.

After resting, Roald was feeling pretty spunky. As we pulled away he barked in Sojo's ear. It was one time too many. Sweet, shy little Sojo whipped her head around and barked right back in his face! Roald was absolutely stunned.

The next morning, Roald gave Sojo's ear another blast. This time Sojo was serious. I watched without interfering as Sojo pounced on him and screamed a tirade of dog abuse in his ear. No matter how hard he pulled back, he couldn't get away from her.

▲ The Nechilik, a ship that once belonged to the Hudson's Bay Company, a famous northern trading company. The Nechilik went aground after striking an uncharted rock in September 1957. It was abandoned, and the entire crew was rescued by another ship.

Finally, she stopped to catch her breath. Roald shook his head as if his ear hurt, which it probably did. Before he could fully recover, she started up again. Roald just fell over on his side and lay still, in a perfect display of dog submission.

My confidence-building program had finally worked! Roald didn't bother Sojo again for the rest of our journey.

Halfway

As we continued across Amundsen Gulf, we alternated between the beach and the sea ice. When the beach became gravelly due to thin snow cover, I tried to switch to the ice. But sometimes the sea ice was rough, which made progress difficult no matter which route I chose.

After a while, the combination of constant wind and rough ice wore me down.

APRIL 20, 1993   +1°F   18 M.P.H. SE   0 MILES, STORM/WHITEOUT

I am frustrated beyond words. The wind continues to blow. It's completely overcast with flat light. It is impossible to see more than a few feet. To travel into the wind through rough ice in flat light would be an exercise in futility. Douggie's leg is sore again today, so maybe it's better that he get a chance to rest. He looks tired. I gave him a burlap bag to sleep on and blocked the area behind him with snow to block out any draft, so he can be as comfortable as I can make him. I know he'll work no matter what because he's so darn tough. But I have to watch out for him.

I feel depressed. All I want is for this trip to be over. I've been in the Arctic since December 3. I'm tired of living in cramped conditions and the same routine every day. This trip is too long with too much time alone. Right now I hate it.

But I have to finish. There is no choice. Now it is for Dottie.

Fortunately, the next day we reached the halfway point. In spite of the terrain and weather, my spirits lifted.

APRIL 21, 1993   0°F   LIGHT WIND   34 MILES

I came to the Harding River, which is where the people in Paulatuk said to turn inland. But to me it looked very punchy, and I thought the dogs would

A Day in the Life of a Dog Musher

Most days on the trail I got up at 6:30 A.M. and fed the dogs, first thing. While they digested their breakfast, I prepared and ate my own. Then I finished dressing, emptied the tent, and packed everything in camp onto the sleds.

At 8:00 A.M., while packing, I recorded the weather measurements. By 8:45 A.M. we were usually under way.

Lunch was served promptly at 1:00 P.M. If I forgot, the dogs would remind me.

We traveled, stopping frequently for breaks, until about 6:00 P.M., when I would start looking for a good place to camp. Around 6:30 P.M. I began setting up camp, after which I fed the dogs, cooked my dinner, ate, and recorded the day's events in my journal.

I tried to be in bed by 9:30 P.M. to get a full nine hours of sleep. Though I usually sleep less at home, on the trail I seem to need an extra hour or two of rest to keep up my energy.

During the darkest days of winter, we normally traveled only a few hours per day, in the twilight between 11:30 A.M. and 2:30 P.M. ☾

have a horrible time going up it, so we kept going. I was told not to come this way—that it's too rocky and no one goes the way I'm now going.

We've come 1,225 miles so far! So we're at the official halfway point. Very nice feeling. Tomorrow we start going downhill, so to speak.

APRIL 23, 1993   -6°F   LIGHT WIND   35 MILES

Good but slow day. Came to a frozen lake and found millions of caribou tracks. And the tracks of a single wolf. Hope the wolf keeps after the caribou and doesn't bother us.

The sun was hot, especially on black Douggie. We just need one more good-weather day and we'll be in Coppermine. I wish I could tell the dogs just how close we are! Then they'd move faster and we could get there faster.

I feel like a solo sailor I once read about who sails alone all over the world. He said he could hardly wait to leave port and get to sea. Then once he got to sea, he could hardly wait to get to port.

In the village of Coppermine, a Native community that seemed to be bustling with activity, I picked up my supplies and spoke at both the elementary school and the College of the Arctic. Temperatures were warm—a little too warm for late April, it seemed to me. If the ice began melting unseasonably early, we might have trouble reaching Repulse Bay before breakup.

When I mentioned my concern to the local wildlife officer, Alex Buchan, he assured me it would turn cold again. As we traveled east toward Bay Chimo, temperatures continued to range from 10°F to 20°F. I tried to quit worrying and enjoy the scenery.

APRIL 30, 1993   +10°F   CLEAR   40 MILES

Not since Demarcation Bay has the Arctic looked so spectacular. Our route across Coronation Gulf took us to a long chain of small islands. The sun had already melted most of the snow away, revealing rugged hillsides of massive, vertical rock formations with enormous piles of giant boulders along the bases. The slate-gray rock contrasts sharply with the snow and makes a pleasant relief for our tired minds.

MAY 1, 1993   +16°F   5 M.P.H. SE   35 MILES

Woke up this morning and it was snowing—wet snow that soaked the tent. For the afternoon I put Anna back in the team and put Lucy up in lead. Usually Lucy hates running lead, but today she didn't seem to mind. I think because there were so many seal holes to find. Lucy likes finding and sniffing them. I saw six seals hauled out.

I have another sore throat, and when I eat, my stomach cramps up. Another gift of my recent visit to civilization. I stay healthy out here but get sick after visiting a town.

MAY 2, 1993   +20°F   36 MILES

We came around the corner of a peninsula and now Bay Chimo is a straight shot of fifty-five miles. We'll be there the day after tomorrow if the ice is smooth.

The water I made in camp tasted salty, which is probably good for my throat. I hope this heat wave goes away. The ice won't last long at these temperatures.

▼ *The team and I resting on the beach in front of a small iceberg about twelve to fourteen feet high and seventy to eighty feet long.*

We arrived in Bay Chimo, or *Umingmaktok* (which means "the place where musk oxen are"), on May 4. I picked up my supplies and decided to splurge by purchasing some food from the store to vary my diet. Ordinarily, one can each of peaches, oranges, strawberries, and stew, plus three cans of orange juice, a

▲ Camp scene in front
of the Coppermine
Mountains, the gentlest
and sunniest part of the
journey. On calm,
sunny days the dogs
were sometimes left
spread out in the evening
to have more room. But
before bed I moved them
behind the sleds to
shelter them from any
breeze that might come
up in the night.

small bottle of aspirin, and six gallons of fuel wouldn't be considered much of a splurge. But in this small, isolated Arctic village, where all store-bought supplies have to be flown in, those few items cost $79.03!

While I was in the store, a number of elders shook my hand in greeting. Our conversation was limited because they spoke no English and I spoke no Inuktituk. Eventually, I found someone who spoke English and arranged for a cache to be taken out about a hundred miles toward Cambridge Bay, to a spot about two miles east of Half Way Point.

Rain

MAY 8, 1993   0 MILES, STORM, BAY CHIMO

It stormed last night worse than any storm I've ever been in. And it rained! It poured. Everything is soaked.

We left Bay Chimo in heavy rain, heading north toward Half Way Point, which lies midway between Bay Chimo and Cambridge Bay. My beaver mitts absorbed the rain water like heavy-duty sponges; my clothes were soaked and my boots became squishy. Then the temperature dropped. Soon I, the dogs, and the entire Arctic were coated with an armor of inch-thick ice. For hours I sat in my tent with the stove blasting away, trying to get back to just being damp, while the dogs licked ice off their fur.

We were prepared for cold and snow—not rain. My boots, parkas, and tent were designed to withstand extreme winds and freezing temperatures. My gear was not waterproof because waterproofing prevents materials from wicking moisture away from the body, and because moisture from rain was not usually a concern at this time of year in the Arctic. The combination of cold temperatures and wet clothing, even in above-freezing temperatures, could prove deadly by leading quickly to hypothermia.

Normally the weather in this part of the Arctic stays cold until July, by which time I had expected to complete the expedition. Now I began to worry seriously about an early breakup. We needed to get across Queen Maud Gulf as soon as possible, while it was still frozen.

Clothing

The basic rule for keeping warm in the Arctic is to keep dry. When temperatures are freezing, as they normally are in the Arctic for most of the year, moisture from rain isn't a concern. Moisture from body perspiration, however, is a constant concern. Expedition clothing is designed to "breathe," to let body moisture wick out and evaporate.

While on the trail I wore several layers of clothing, which I could add or subtract to adjust for the temperature. Beneath my jeans and T-shirt I wore two pairs of lightweight, synthetic-fiber long underwear. Over my jeans and sweater I pulled on a pair of bib overalls, insulated with one inch of a foam-rubber–type material. On top of that I wore a heavy-duty parka, also insulated with the foam-rubber material.

My hat was helmet-style and lined with the same type of insulation, with a baseball bill and chin strap. I wore a pair of synthetic gloves under a pair of wool gloves, then covered both with mittens filled with the foam-rubber insulation.

My feet stayed warm encased in one pair of synthetic-fiber socks, covered by two pairs of wool socks. Over those I wore midcalf boots made of a heavy-duty outer fabric with a removable foam-rubber liner.

Then something even worse happened—terrible enough to make all my other worries seem unimportant.

Douggie Disappears

MAY 11, 1993   +34°F   15 M.P.H. E

Just as we were almost ready to leave camp, a pair of caribou emerged from behind a nearby rock. Douggie was standing beside me as I prepared to put his harness on. He ran about twenty feet toward them and stopped. I called him back, but he just stood there. I called him again. He looked at me, then at the caribou, then at me.

Douggie had had enough of being Mr. Well-Disciplined Hard-Working Sled Dog and took off in pursuit of the fleeing caribou.

I couldn't believe it! Douggie, my pride and joy, had just run off. As soon as I hooked up the rest of the team, we took off after Douggie.

His tracks disappeared in the hard-packed snow and slick ice of the surrounding hills on the Kent Peninsula. Hours of searching stretched into days. By the third day, I was beside myself with worry and fear. What if a pack of wolves found him? One lone dog wouldn't stand a chance. What could he possibly find to eat? He might become completely lost in the hills and starve to death. If the worst happened, and we couldn't find him, or found him dead, how could we possibly continue the expedition without him?

These fears swirled through me constantly as we searched. After the third day, without once seeing Douggie or even his tracks, I decided to go to the nearest village, about a hundred miles away, to organize a search party.

In Cambridge Bay I posted a $500 reward for finding Douggie.

MAY 15, 1993

Called Alice Holinger and asked her to put Douggie on the prayer chain. I feel so angry, upset, sad, disappointed. I was so proud of the fact that I'd never lost a dog on a trip. Now I've lost my best dog, my leader, my biggest, strongest, most experienced. I've lost my Douglas.

I searched by snowmobile with two local men, Mark and Alfred, for two more days. But the sun was melting the snow so rapidly that any tracks Douggie might have left were now gone. There was no sign of Douggie anywhere.

MAY 17, 1993

I talked to Alice again. She tells me I must find it within myself to accept what has happened and go on. "Don't quit."

I want to quit so badly. But Douglas may have given his life for this trip. His death should have some meaning.

Though part of me still had trouble believing it, the fact was that Douggie was gone. No amount of tears or guilt or grief would change that. I knew I had to accept it and find the strength to continue. I didn't know if it was even *possible* to finish without him. But we owed Douggie so much that I felt that we had to try.

The next day, I was sad and depressed as I prepared to leave Cambridge Bay. I knew that once we left, we'd never see Douggie again.

Just as we were leaving, I saw some people I recognized from Bay Chimo. They smiled and said, "We saw your dog near Half Way Point." I described him, and they assured me it was Douggie.

Douggie was alive! I quickly changed plans and headed back toward Half Way Point to find him. The dogs were as fired up as I was. In twenty-four hours we covered seventy-two miles, hoping all the way to find him.

MAY 20, 1993

We reached the place known as Half Way Point. Rounding the corner I saw nothing but an empty bay. I stood there, looking around and listening to the never-ending wind. Where was Douggie? I checked by some empty barrels where he was seen, and I found his tracks. But they were covered by many other tracks, and I couldn't figure out anything.

The next day, just as I was about to give in to total despair, I heard from a passing snowmobiler that Douggie had walked into Bay Chimo that morning. Every snowmobiler in town had roared after him—and the $500 reward. It took two more days before I was finally able to meet up with the family who claimed him. By then, Douggie had been gone for twelve days, and we had traveled about three hundred extra miles searching for him (not counted in the expedition total). When we met on the trail, Douggie was in a cargo box on the trailer sled behind the family's snowmobile.

MAY 23, 1993

I walked slowly to the sled box and looked inside. There sat Douggie! He was really alive!

He was also in a state of shock. Too much had happened to him. He sat there staring straight ahead, not even recognizing me. I reached in and hugged him and kissed him on top of his head.

Henry, Lena, and their daughter, Karen, helped me lift Douggie from the sled box. I slowly led him over to the team. He just stood there as though he'd never seen these dogs before. Ever so slowly the entire team gathered around Douggie. Everyone carefully sniffed him. Their tails wagged slowly. They seemed truly touched that he was back and were very gentle with him.

Then slowly Douggie's face changed. A look of recognition began to come over his face. His tail wagged very, very slowly. I knew he would be okay.

Douggie-Dog was tough. I wished he could talk and tell us what had happened to him.

Douggie was very thin and would need time to recuperate. But considering what he'd been through, he looked okay. The next day he ate six meals in twelve hours! I fed him as much as he wanted.

By now we'd used most of the cache from Half Way Point. In Cambridge Bay I arranged to have supplies taken east near Whitebear Point. When Douggie seemed to feel better, we started traveling again, along the southern shore of Queen Maud Gulf. I tried to take it easy on him by frequently putting Anna or Lucy in lead.

MAY 25, 1993   +28°F   30 MILES

The snow is terribly coarse and grainy. I have to keep booties on everyone most of the time.

The snow is getting ready to melt quickly now. Coming through the neck of the Kent Peninsula, onto Queen Maud Gulf, we sledded over many places where there was bare tundra—and even mud. The runners get stuck in the mud, and the tundra drags the sleds down.

Douggie continues to eat and eat. He even stole some of Lucy's food tonight! She let him do it, which is even more of a surprise.

Normally the dogs are not allowed to steal food from one another. But this time was different. I'll never know for sure, but I believe that I witnessed an act of simple canine compassion when Lucy turned her head and pretended she didn't see what he was doing. It was as if Lucy understood that Douggie, her friend and teammate, needed the food more than she did.

MAY 26, 1993 +26°F 10 M.P.H. N 33 MILES

Everyone did well. Douggie and Anna were in lead most of the day. I had to give many commands to sled through some rough ice, and that started to stress Anna out. So I moved Lucy up and Anna back. I petted her and told her she did a good job. She seemed to relax immediately right before my eyes.

It's so warm the dogs sleep on their sides and don't even curl up.

MAY 27, 1993 +28°F 0 MILES, REST DAY

Rested here by the cache near Whitebear Point all day, to give Douggie a break so he regains some strength. I can use the rest, too, as all the stress and lack of sleep caused by Douggie's misadventure have left me drained. Tomorrow we set out for Gjoa Haven, 260 miles away.

That night I couldn't help worrying. To reach Gjoa Haven we had to cross 260 miles of sea ice over Queen Maud Gulf. If temperatures kept climbing, we might find ourselves out in the middle of the gulf, mushing through slush rather than ice.

I tried to reassure myself. It was far too early for the sea ice to melt. Normally it would stay frozen at least until the end of June, or into July. Surely this was just a warm spell that wouldn't last. After all the difficulties we'd already come through, we could make it across Queen Maud. I refused to let myself think about the steadily rising temperatures I'd been recording in my journal.

I knew one thing, though: we had to get moving. The sooner, and the faster, the better.

Queen Maud Misery

MAY 28, 1993 +34°F 15 M.P.H. NE 33 MILES

Pretty good day today. We made excellent time over the sea ice to Whitebear Point, crossed the narrow peninsula about four miles south of the point, and continued back onto Queen Maud Gulf. The snow is very wet and sticky. It's going to melt soon. I hope it starts cooling off more in the night.

The big problem right now is the dog food bucket. It's been heated so many times over the stove that it's been cooked through. It has three leaks in the bottom and a leak on the side. I duct-taped the side. But the bottom is a problem. Each night now I have to position the bucket just right over the burner so the three leaks don't flood the burner and put it out.

All the dog lines are frayed. There aren't any replacements left. We are a ragtag-looking crew.

MAY 29, 1993   +42°F   3 M.P.H.   NE   33 MILES

Horrible, frightening day. We set out at 9:00 A.M. heading east in very thick fog. After about an hour we came to a lead that none of us saw until Anna and Douggie crashed through a snow bridge that went over it.

I jumped on the brake with both feet and smashed the snowhook into the soft snow. The sled stopped about four feet from the edge. The edge was soft and rotten. Douggie and Anna pulled themselves up on the ice on the far side. Robert was in the water with his front feet up on the ice, but he couldn't get the rest of himself up because his harness was pulling him back. Sojo was on the edge of the lead with her harness pulled over her head, trying to keep from being dragged in. The remaining four dogs were freaked.

I pulled on the lines, which forced Robert to back up and pulled Douggie and Anna into the water. They were scared and had a hard time getting out of the water on my side of the lead, even though I was pulling on their lines. Finally they were all out. I immediately petted everyone and talked to them in a happy, singsong voice. Everyone seemed to calm down.

Later the fog closed in around us and the ice got rough. We really got slowed down. The snow between the ice chunks was now three to six inches of heavy slush. The dogs had a very hard time pulling through it.

At 5:00 P.M. Anna started sitting down every few minutes. I think she was tired. She doesn't pace herself and wears herself out by working so hard. When I tell her to go, she goes. She is as tough as Douggie. I have so much respect for these dogs.

My big fear is that breakup is here four to six weeks early and we may not be able to finish the trip. I feel tense and scared. We've come so far only to—maybe—fail.

MAY 30, 1993   +42°F   5 M.P.H.   N   26 MILES

A real tough day today. We're driving through five inches of thick slush. Very hard on the dogs. I hope when we get off the ice onto Hat Island it gets better.

It rained all day.

We rested every forty-five minutes or so. The dogs are straining so hard to move the sled that we have to stop that often. I feel sorry for them.

▶ *Heading out over the melting sea ice of Queen Maud Gulf, fifty miles from land in 66°F temperature.*

I'm absolutely certain now that we're not going to get to Repulse Bay this spring. Maybe not even Pelly Bay. Breakup is here very early and we're going to fail. I feel sort of scared and panicked. My stomach hurts all the time now from worry.

I don't know what I'll do if I fail. Somehow I have to come through.

This morning as I lay listening to the rain striking the tent, the dogs started to bark. I looked out and saw eight Canada geese sitting on the snow about a hundred yards away.

The sight of the geese stunned me. Their migration back to the Arctic is usually a welcome event, embodying the return of life to the land. But we were still almost fifty miles from shore, camped on rapidly rotting ice. To me, their arrival meant that time had run out—perhaps, even, that death was approaching. If we couldn't reach shore before the sea ice melted, we might die.

I felt completely powerless, but surprisingly calm. As I watched them, it occurred to me that the birds had not come here to die. Each of them had started life in the Arctic and now was returning to live and give life. The thought made me feel a little less despondent. I could only do as those birds were doing—live one day at a time and try to survive.

MAY 31, 1993   +48°F   28 MILES

It's very hot, and I hope we make it into Gjoa Haven before the ice collapses under us. We ran through slush and standing water. The water tastes salty to me, but the dogs lick it some.

We took fifteen rest breaks. During the last one-and-a-half hours Douggie didn't work, just walked along, and Anna led. By the end of the day we were all staggering.

We jumped across a two-and-a-half-foot-wide lead, and all went well, except Roald, who went in completely. He was crying and whining so pitifully. I felt so sorry for him. I tried to help pull him out but lost my grip. Then he went to the other side of the lead and pulled himself out.

I quickly got everything over to the east side of the lead, then petted Roald and told him what a good dog he was. He seemed to like that. Douggie didn't mind jumping over the lead, even though he'd been dunked the other day.

We have to put in long days because we travel so slowly through the slush. I don't know what else to do. We have to get to Gjoa Haven on King William Island while there is still ice to get to shore on. It's going very fast.

We came to one very thin area of upheaval in the ice. Suddenly Anna jumped to the left and the whole team went that way. The sled sort of sank in the mush, but the dogs, with their incredible instincts and ability, got us through safely.

Today at lunch we were resting south of Hat Island and I could hear the ice grinding in Requisite Channel. I'm so glad I chose to go on the south side of Hat Island, not the north. The shifting ice over there must be very dangerous right now. We ended our lunch break five minutes early as I couldn't stand listening to the noise. It seemed as though the sound was crushing my dream.

How much do I want not to fail?

▼ Thermometer reading 66°F on Queen Maud Gulf as breakup begins, four to six weeks early.

JUNE 1, 1993   +68°F   12 MILES

I'm changing the schedule again. We started at 4:00 A.M., when it was 34°F, and sledded until 9:10 A.M. The ice was bad to start; then some good; then brutal for the last mile. Ahead looks equally bad. But I can see an island ahead.

We stopped at 9:10 because of the heat and exhaustion. When it cools off we'll go on. It's getting scary out here on the gulf in this heat. Water standing everywhere.

We have to cross seven miles of sea ice to get to the islands I see ahead; then sea ice and land; then one last stretch of sea ice before reaching the Adelaide Peninsula. I pray this sea ice doesn't explode on us before we get there.

I feel scared.

We'll travel all night, when it's coolest. But I don't think it will even get down to freezing.

No camp today. Just slept on the sled and the dogs slept in slush.

JUNE 2, 1993   10 M.P.H. S   18 MILES

Nightmare day. I am exhausted. We're running into bad ice, running out of dog food. It has got to get better. God, it has got to get better.

JUNE 4, 1993   15 M.P.H. N   0 MILES

Didn't travel today. It was raining all day and very warm. We are exhausted. The ice is so soft we can't travel on it. So we wait in hopes that it will firm up. We're on a tiny island about one-quarter by one-half mile in size. We're running out of food, so I hunted seal, but missed every shot.

JUNE 5, 1993   +34°F   10 M.P.H. N

Today is Douggie's birthday. Started out at 1:00 A.M. The ice is firm enough to travel on but still soft and slushy. The dogs didn't want to travel through the slush. It was hard to get them off the island onto the slushy ice. We traveled until 10:00 A.M. Anna zigs and zags around a lot, going from snow patch to snow patch.

My journal entries for this portion of the journey end here. At this point, the dogs and I were struggling so hard for survival that I didn't have the energy to keep writing.

This is what I remember:

Standing on the first island, I thought very seriously about giving up. I had an ELT (emergency locator transmitter), which, if triggered, would eventually bring a helicopter to rescue me.

But I knew that it would rescue only me. Wilderness helicopter rescues are extremely expensive. The helicopter would not make extra return flights to transport the dogs unless I could pay the bill. And I could not.

Neither could I abandon my dogs to die. I put the ELT in the very bottom of my sled bag and decided we would make it together, or not at all.

From then on it rained every day. The temperature never dropped below freezing again. The heat continued to be so unbelievable that I took a photo of my thermometer at 66°F as proof. The ice broke up into huge chunks. Sometimes we had to jump from one chunk to another, crossing small cracks, one to two feet wide, in the semi-frozen sea. The dogs became fearless. They learned to cross quickly.

The ice was also full of holes, which kept growing bigger and bigger. I figured out that if the water standing in the hole was gray, there was ice in the bottom of the hole, and no matter how deep the water, we could sled over it. If the water was blue, the ice was gone from the hole, and we sledded around it. To check the condition of the ice in a hole, I jabbed it with my ice probe.

I no longer set up camp. We just stopped and rested when we were too tired to go on: I on top of the sled, the dogs lying in the slush. I didn't have to melt snow anymore, either. There was water, water everywhere! Plenty for all of us, and plenty to spare.

My food, which was supposed to stay frozen, spoiled. I was reduced to eating only precooked sausage, at about one-quarter of my usual daily food ration.

Thank goodness I'd wrapped all the dog food in large plastic bags! I managed to keep their food dry. Even so, I was forced to cut the dogs' portions in half because we were running out of supplies. Douggie was the only exception. He'd lost too much weight already and needed full rations. Still, Douggie, along with everyone else, lost weight.

I no longer rode the sled. We moved so slowly that I could easily keep up by walking, and I didn't want the dogs to have to pull me. My boots were always full of water and seemed to weigh about ten pounds each. Inside the boots, my wet, wrinkled feet chafed raw from the constant moisture, but, surprisingly, they stayed warm.

One day stands out in my mind as perhaps the worst of all these days that were nothing but "worst." We were crossing a pressure ridge, which in reality turned out to be a pile of slush. The dogs crossed safely, but the front sled got stuck. When I tried to push on the sled handle, I fell through the slush into the water. Suddenly my pants began filling with water. Just as suddenly, I was sinking.

My head was already below the level of the ice. I managed to grab hold of the sled runner and screamed at the dogs, "All right!" But they couldn't budge the sled.

I felt myself getting heavier and heavier as water seeped into more of my clothing. If I didn't get out of that water immediately, I was going to drown.

▼ *Scooping meltwater from the sea ice of Queen Maud Gulf during breakup.*

I remember looking at a line dangling down the side of my sled and thinking *I'll never reach it. And if I do, I'm not sure I have the strength to hang on.* The sled runners, I noticed, were sinking into the slush. My weight was pulling the sled down.

I didn't think after that, but simply lunged. Somehow I managed to grab the line. Hand over hand, I pulled myself up until I was lying on the ice.

It was raining, and my glasses were covered with mist. I was beyond fear, beyond panic. I was utterly exhausted and suddenly furious. I hauled myself up onto my feet, raised my fists toward the sky, and screamed at God like a crazy woman: "Don't you ever play with my life like that again, do you hear me? Either kill me or leave me alone!"

And in that instant, it stopped raining. I was startled out of my fury. Was God actually listening?

I don't know for sure. But I do know that the rain stopped. I remember it very clearly.

And so we continued.

One day I heard a plane land a few miles away on King William Island. I knew there was a DEW Line station there at Gladman Point, and I was elated to know there were people. We would go there and get some emergency supplies. We desperately needed food. Then, with luck, we could continue to Gjoa Haven.

The island became a beacon for me. Somehow we had to get there. Not only were we half starving, I could see that Douggie's health was failing. His ordeal in the hills had cost him more physical strength than I'd realized; his stamina was fading.

Each day Anna took over more as leader. She was simply outstanding. Now, when I needed her the most, she came through. Douggie stayed in lead, but I didn't ask him to do anything except walk along. I would have liked to let him ride in the sled, but I was afraid to. Frequently, now, the water was as deep as two feet. The sled often floated like an unseaworthy boat, easily tipping. Douggie was so weak that I feared he might drown before I could right the sled.

It was light all the time now in the Arctic. We stopped only for brief breaks to rest when we couldn't go on. The entire week passed as a blur of slush, water, and exhaustion.

Somehow, at last, we approached land. Genuine solid earth was in sight. But as we neared the shore of King William Island, the water between kept getting deeper and deeper. It looked like we might run out of ice before we made it to shore.

About a hundred yards from land the dogs began swimming. The sled was floating and tipping. If it began to sink, and if there was no ice for me to stand on beneath the water, I couldn't save all eight dogs from being pulled under and drowning.

I veered to the left. Thankfully, the water became shallower. The dogs started walking again, and I relaxed a little—until Anna fell through a hidden seal hole.

By now the seal holes in this area were filled with sea water. At this moment, the tide was churning the water into a whirlpool. Anna thrashed around frantically, trying to pull herself out of the swirling water. Her terrified eyes met mine, begging for help.

I rushed up and grabbed her harness to lift her out. But the ice around her was so thin I began to break through. I knew that if I fell in and got sucked under the ice, no one would survive. I ran back to the sled, my mind racing.

"Douggie!" I screamed. "Haw, Douggie! Haw!"

Weak as he was, Douggie somehow found the strength to pull to the left. As he did, the other dogs seemed to understand what was needed. Suddenly, all seven dogs were pulling to the left. Together they dragged Anna out of the freezing water and saved her life.

I watched in amazement as Anna stood up, shook herself off, and went straight back to work as if nothing had happened. What a fearless, tough-minded dog!

We sledded along the edge of the ice, next to the water. I could see that, in fact, the ice did not reach all the way to shore. After a lot of searching I found a little peninsula that stretched off the island to within three feet of us. From there we jumped, swam, and crawled our way onto dry land.

Decision

For several minutes, all of us simply lay motionless on the cold earth of King William Island. The dogs seemed as relieved as I was to be on solid ground. There was no snow on the beach, only gravel.

▼ *Happy to be alive, and holding my satellite navigator, which displays a readout of the coordinates for Gladman Point, where we reached land after crossing Queen Maud Gulf. Note the building in the background, amount of daylight, and lack of snow cover. The dog is Anna.*

After a while I got up and walked toward the Gladman Point DEW Line station about a quarter-mile away. As I got near, my heart sank to my knees. The station was boarded up. I could see that no one was there. No food for us; no help for Douggie.

I walked around the site in disbelief, staring at the boarded windows. Gradually I became aware of a low hum. It was a droning sound I vaguely recognized: the noise of a generator.

I started checking every building. About a half-mile farther I found a smaller, newer site that appeared to be completely automated and powered by the generator.

The door to one building was open. Inside I found a room about the size of a very small bedroom. On the opposite wall were locked doors. On the wall to my left I saw a surveillance camera—and a telephone.

As I stood there, numb with hunger and exhaustion, trying to force my mind to think about what to do, the phone rang!

I almost jumped straight out of my boots. Feeling completely unnerved, I picked up the receiver. A man from Goose Bay, Ontario, asked me who in the world I was and what in the world I was doing there!

Somehow I managed to explain my situation. Then I quickly made a decision I'd been agonizing over for days as we'd plodded along. I asked for help. I asked him to find someone I could hire from Gjoa Haven, the nearest village, to bring us in by snowmobile.

Next to my decision to leave Cambridge Bay without Douggie, this was the hardest decision I had to make on the expedition. But by then I felt there really was no choice. It would be madness to continue on the sea "ice." It was almost gone. On land, only pockets of mushy snow remained. Walking overland wouldn't work because we couldn't move the sleds with all our supplies over bare ground. Besides, the rivers had already thawed and were sending torrents of water down to the sea. I knew I couldn't get the dogs across those rivers safely.

Even if we could somehow travel the sixty miles to Gjoa Haven, it would take at least one week. Douggie looked like he wouldn't survive another week without proper nourishment and rest.

I turned endless ideas over and over in my head, trying to figure out a way to carry on. Each time I reached the same conclusion: Douggie would most likely die if I tried to continue.

After all we'd been through, it was a painful blow to quit. I felt profoundly sad to find my dream disintegrating around me. But there was no alternative. I knew in my heart that Douggie was more important than my dream.

Accepting the reality of our situation was tough. But I've never regretted my decision.

Two days later, on June 9, Mark Tootiak and his son Jason showed up on two snowmobiles, each pulling a trailer sled. Melting ice and open water had forced them into countless detours, stretching the six-hour trip they'd expected into two days. Now they, too, were out of food and hungry.

Mark took one look at Douggie and saw that something was wrong. By then Douggie's eyes were dull, and he lay on his side, almost lifeless. Mark, Jason, and I shared my last chunk of sausage and then wasted no time loading the dogs into a large box attached to Jason's trailer sled. My sleds and gear were towed behind Mark's snowmobile. After months of silently, laboriously crossing the Arctic by muscle power, we were soon roaring over the tundra by snowmobile. Because most of the snow was gone, we drove over a patchwork of bare ground and slush.

Rivers thirty or more feet wide had flooded the sea ice in many places. To cross them, we machined south until we found a place where the water was flowing through cracks in the ice, but not flooding the ice. These leads were about ten to twelve feet wide. Mark and Jason approached a lead, then began driving in circles, going faster and faster. Suddenly they headed for the lead at breakneck speed and flew right over.

Riding behind Jason on his trailer sled, the dogs and I flew over behind them. Amazingly, we never fell into any of the leads or even got wet. I learned later that lead-jumping was a favorite sport in this part of the world, and could only feel grateful that it was so.

Twelve hours later, still wet, half starving, and total strangers, we arrived with Jason and Mark in the Inuit village of Gjoa Haven.

Rest and Recovery

When we arrived in Gjoa Haven, the dogs and I were scarecrow-thin, weak, and exhausted. I parked the team on the beach by the edge of town, behind a two-story house in which Mark, a Royal Canadian Mounted Police officer, and his wife, Naavee, lived. They kindly gave me a place to stay while I figured out what to do.

I went back to the beach, sat on a boulder, and tried to think. I was stuck in Gjoa Haven, an Inuit community of about 850 people located on King William Island in the Nunavut territory of Canada. No roads connected Gjoa Haven to the rest of the world. The only way in or out of town during breakup was by airplane. I had seven dollars in my pocket, few provisions, and a sick lead dog. My problems seemed monumental.

What was I going to do? Obviously it was time to quit. Give up! What else could I do except get on the next plane and head home?

But wait a minute . . . that would cost a lot of money, which I didn't have.

Okay. So maybe I couldn't leave town. Maybe I couldn't quit. Maybe I'd have to find some way to continue. But how? The ice was melting, and mushing was impossible.

It just wasn't fair! We'd worked so hard, endured so much. Now it seemed as though everything was for naught. This journey, the dream of my life, was unraveling before my eyes. For quite a while I sat on that boulder, staring blankly past the dogs and feeling depressed.

Finally, I got tired of it. I told myself to get a grip.

You're not going to quit, and you're not going on, at least not now. Think this through. I would handle this problem the same way I'd handled every other problem I'd encountered on the trip: one step at a time.

First I had to make a plan. That was the easy part.

I decided we would stay in Gjoa Haven for the summer, rest, and wait for the ice to return in the fall. Then we would finish the last five hundred miles of the trip.

▼ *Gjoa Haven seen from a hill beside the town.*

But how would I make that plan work?

To begin with, we needed food. The school, where I'd sent some supplies, was already closed for the summer. Naavee quickly found the janitor to open it up. Soon I'd dragged our supplies over to the beach where the dogs were tethered. I got a bucket of warm water from Naavee and started soaking dog food.

Instantly the dogs perked up. Sixteen eyes focused intently on that bucket. As if someone in the sky were pulling a string, the entire team rose to a sitting position. One by one, they began to drool. Soon long, sticky strings of drool hung all the way to their toes.

To a passerby this might have looked rather disgusting. To me it looked beautiful! It was a sign that they were still healthy enough to have an appetite. But I was very worried about Douggie. Though he drooled along with the rest of them, his eyes were dull, and he was much thinner than the others. If he'd passed too far into starvation, he might never recover fully.

The dogs hadn't eaten full rations for a week. So when the food was ready, I fed out only half of a normal ration, about two cupfuls, to each dog. I didn't want them to gorge themselves and get sick. Everyone except Douggie wolfed down their food in an instant. Douggie took one bite, swallowed, and then stopped. As he stood staring at his food, I held my breath.

Slowly, he took another bite. And another. After each bite he stopped to rest. Long after the others had finished, Douggie finally ate the last bit. Then, like the rest of the team, he lay down to sleep.

It was a lovely day, with a beautiful blue sky and no wind. As I sat alone on the beach, watching Douggie sleep, I came to accept what I'd refused to believe when we were fighting for our lives out on the ice. Douggie couldn't finish the trip this season. He was just too tired and thin to make it. If we had tried to struggle on, Douggie would likely have died. And I knew that no amount of joy at succeeding could have erased the pain of losing Douggie.

I began to see that being stuck in Gjoa Haven wasn't a problem, but a solution. Douggie needed a very long rest and lots of good food to regain his strength. And now I had all summer to give him that.

Half an hour later I fed the dogs another half ration and let them rest again.

News of my plight traveled quickly in this small town. The very next morning I was invited to stay in an empty house in the village. I couldn't believe my good fortune!

This one-story house, typical for the Arctic, had all the modern comforts I could hope for: electricity, television, telephone, oil heat, bathroom, real beds, and a complete kitchen. I moved in immediately and gratefully. The first thing I did in my new home was collapse on the couch for a long nap. Apparently I had some recuperating to do, too.

I learned that dog teams weren't allowed to stay inside the village, for reasons of noise and sanitation, but were kept on the far side of a creek on the west end of town. Soon I moved the dogs to a suitable spot out of the wind in "dogtown," which was only about a quarter-mile walk from where I was staying.

Now that we had a place to stay, my most pressing problem was food. Our supplies would run out quickly. How would I feed the dogs?

The answer was right in front of my eyes. Codfish were abundant in Amundsen Bay, the small bay on which Gjoa Haven was located. Though the ice was now completely gone from the waters around King William Island, Amundsen Bay would stay covered for several more weeks. I spent each day of those next three weeks fishing through leads in the ice to feed my dogs. Sometimes I fished alone, but often I fished with the local kids or a new-found friend named Carey Cahill. Her husband, Charlie, had found me the house to stay in.

One day, though, as Carey and I were heading toward the bay, a boy about ten years old ran up to us, shouting, "Don't go out there! The ice isn't safe anymore."

Now how would I feed the dogs? The ice was too thin to walk on any longer; yet it still clogged the shore, so I couldn't fish from the beach. Charlie suggested putting a request for fish on the noon radio broadcast, when local messages were read for everyone to hear.

I wrote out my request and dropped it off at the station. At home I turned on the radio. Just after noon I heard: "Pam Flowers could use some help feeding her dogs today, if anyone has some fish or other meat they don't need." Immediately I heard my name again, but this time the message was read in Inuktituk.

Within fifteen minutes the phone rang. A young woman said she had some fish in her freezer that I could have. I got directions to her house and immediately set about baking a batch of cookies.

I had no money to offer in exchange, but Charlie had told me that no one would take my money even if I'd had any! They might, however, appreciate something baked. And indeed, the cookies were a big hit. When I knocked on the door, I was invited in for tea, my cookies, and a visit. I left with eight large arctic char.

▲ *People in Gjoa Haven helping me fish to feed my dogs. There was never a shortage of fish, or people willing to catch them.*

▼ *Playing hockey after school on a frozen lake by Gjoa Haven in October. Note the almost complete lack of snow and trees in this Arctic desert.*

The next two weeks were hard. The ice moved out of the bay, but so did the codfish. Fishing was poor. Yet every time I failed to get enough fish to feed the dogs, a single message on the radio brought food for another one or two days. Much of the fish I received came from the Qitsualik family, who lived at the end of my road, just before the creek that separated the village from "dogtown." After a while they stopped calling and simply left fish out for me on a fish-cleaning table beside their house. I gladly baked cookies and muffins regularly to deliver to this kind family.

Soon arctic char, which taste somewhat like salmon, arrived in the bay. They were harder to catch than cod, but that only made Carey and me more determined to catch them. Already I could see that, with plenty of rest and food, Douggie was slowly beginning to regain his health. When I wasn't fishing or baking or taking care of the dogs, I raided the garbage dump for pieces of scrap wood. Eventually I pieced together a small house for each dog.

One Wednesday I learned that I had to leave the house I was living in—by Friday! I panicked. What would I do? I called Margie, a neighbor farther down the road. She told me not to worry and made a few phone calls.

I'd always heard that the Inuit people share whatever they have and take care of everyone in their communities. I was experiencing this generosity and concern firsthand. Now the Qitsualik family, who had kindly given me so many fish, gave me a home.

I nervously knocked on the door, and Salomie opened it. A very pleasant-looking woman, about five-foot-four, with long, black hair and a big smile, she waved me into the house. I followed her down the hall and into a spacious, tidy bedroom with a window, all to myself. It was more than I had any reason to hope for.

I met Salomie's eleven-year-old son, Sean; fourteen-year-old daughter, Aida; husband, Gideon; and baby, Naomi, whom they had just adopted that very day. Their home was very similar to the house I'd been living in, except this house had four bedrooms. Aida and Sean spoke both Inuktituk and English. Salomie and Gideon didn't speak English, and I didn't speak Inuktituk; so we used hand gestures and pantomime to communicate. When we failed, we turned to the kids, who translated and got us straightened out.

As a loner, I was a bit uncomfortable living with five people, but I worked very hard at not letting that show. Not even once did I want to offend these kind people who'd taken me in. I baked cookies, muffins, and bread, and did my best to help Salomie prepare lunch, which was often a delicious caribou soup.

I wanted to contribute to my new family's income, but as a foreigner in Canada I couldn't get a job. Store-bought food in the Arctic is very expensive. One small can of peaches, for example, cost $2.05 at that time. So I called good friends Lori and Doug Nichols, in Edmonton, Alberta, and they agreed to send several cases of food through the mail. I paid for the food with my credit card.

The first thing to arrive was canned fruit, which made my family very happy. It was a treat they loved but couldn't afford often. We feasted on canned peaches and pineapple. Later, we received the ingredients for spaghetti and macaroni and cheese.

Summer passed peacefully and rather quickly. Before I knew it, fall and freeze-up arrived. The dogs had gained back all the weight they'd lost. Douggie's eyes brightened, and his health returned. I began training so we could finish the expedition.

By early December the sea ice was thick and strong. I began visiting my friends around Gjoa Haven to say good-bye. I'd decided to leave on December 5. Most people thought that was foolish, because on that day the sun would set for six weeks. No one traveled in the dark season, they said; it would be too cold, dark, and windy. I should wait for the sun to return.

But I figured I already knew about the Arctic's cold, dark, and wind. We had traveled through plenty of it to get this far. I was ready to go, and so were the dogs. Typically, no amount of reasoning could convince me otherwise.

On December 5, 1993, after saying a final farewell to my adoptive family, we left the village that had taken care of us for so many months and set out across Amundsen Bay on our own once again.

Back on the Trail

We headed along the coast back to Gladman Point, where we'd halted the expedition the previous spring, to officially resume our journey there.

DECEMBER 5, 1993   -34°F   9 M.P.H.   N   10 MILES
        Finally got off at 11:00 A.M. Hard pulling for the dogs because we have a big load. That won't last, because we're going to put in a cache at the southeast end of Todd Island. My plan is to then go west to Gladman Point, where we got picked up by Mark and Jason Tootiak. I'll document our arrival there and then start back east. There will be no holes in this expedition.
        The sun peeked over the horizon for just about an hour and stayed orange. I wonder if we'll see it tomorrow? It's nice to be out here again with the dogs. Although I must say, I miss the people and all their smiles.

At Todd Island the next day I set a cache beside an *inuksuk*, a stack of rocks used to indicate a direction or specific location. It was one of many I'd seen in the area.

The cold weather was causing the sea ice to fissure. As the ice contracted and expanded, the dogs barked and growled at the loud pops and groans. That day we crossed eight cracks. Fortunately, none was more than a foot and a half wide. This early in the season I didn't expect any major problems with large leads. I could see the salt water already freezing over in the bottoms of the cracks.

DECEMBER 6, 1993   -27°F   15 M.P.H.   N   13 MILES
        At first Anna didn't like the cracks, but Douggie just dragged her over them. By the end of our three hours of traveling she was shooting right over them without any problem. The dogs are already working well again as a team. It's a real pleasure watching them pull.

DECEMBER 8, 1993   -25°F   BREEZE N   21 MILES

I almost turned into Douglas Bay because it's so big and I thought it was the entrance to Simpson Strait, which will take us to Gladman Point. Douglas the dog did not want to turn into Douglas the bay! And he was right, again. We stayed on course, crossing a couple of pressure ridges that were only two feet high, and four cracks two feet wide. The sun never really rose; it just sent a sort of computer-looking bunch of orange squares over the horizon and went away after about half an hour.

We made twenty-six miles. I'm still nervous about the cold. I seem to start all my trips being afraid of the cold, and then the fear just goes away. I guess I have a good respect for what cold can do, and I need to reassure myself that the dogs and I can handle it okay.

At Gladman Point I took a picture of us, this time with a background of twilight and snow, to prove beyond anyone's doubts that we resumed the expedition from the same place we'd left off the previous spring. The landscape looked familiar, but very different from last spring. I thought about how sick Douggie had been then, how exhausted and emaciated we'd all been, and was again so glad I'd decided to temporarily halt the expedition.

▲ *Gladman Point. Behind me is the building in the photo we took when we first reached Gladman Point and had to stop. Note the very low light, typical pink sky after the final sunset, and increased snow cover.*

■   101

After snapping the photo, we turned around and headed back on our trail toward the Todd Island cache. We were officially under way again, with only about 440 miles left to reach Repulse Bay.

DECEMBER 10, 1993   -31°F   10 M.P.H. S/N   17 MILES

    The dogs headed back along yesterday's trail in a whiteout. I can't see much of the trail, but they seem to be able to stay right on it without any problem. I guess the nose knows. The dogs stopped at precisely 1:00 P.M. and looked back at me to see if I was getting their lunch out of the sled bag. How do they know what time it is? They do this every day! They certainly have gotten back into that schedule pretty fast.

The next day we found our cache beside the inuksuk. As we camped that night, I couldn't help missing my friends in Gjoa Haven.

DECEMBER 11, 1993   -31°F   15 M.P.H. N/NE   23 MILES

    It's sort of lonely camping here, when Gjoa Haven is just a day's sledding north. If I were at the Qitsualiks' I'd probably be dining on caribou tongue tonight. Oh, well. We have to stay on track and not think about what could be, but what is and will be.

    No raisins in my food rations tonight. This is the first mistake I've ever found in my rations.

Crossing Rasmussen Basin, we encountered lots of rubble ice, with patches of flat, easy ice in between. The dogs became frustrated with all the stopping and starting, but there wasn't any way around it.

DECEMBER 13, 1993   -31°F   15 M.P.H. S   19 MILES

    Good ice, bad ice, good ice, bad ice. All day we kept getting stuck. Douggie followed commands and got us through, but the sled kept getting stuck. The pulling was hard from the cold and bad ice.

    Had a fuel leak in my stove generator but got it fixed. Don't like stove problems out here. Hoping to reach Pelly Bay by 12/21.

DECEMBER 14, 1993   -30°F   25 M.P.H. S   0 MILES, STORM

    No travel today. The wind seems to suck warmth right out of a body. The dogs lie hunkered down behind the overturned sleds. They show no desire to get up. Can't blame them.

We have about 150 miles left to Pelly Bay, lots of food and supplies. But storms always give cause for some worry.

DECEMBER 15, 1993   -12°F   BREEZE N   21 MILES

More bad ice, hard pulling through this stuff. But the dogs are doing well after a day of rest. The stove isn't running very well for some reason. I don't know what is wrong. I hope it holds out.

The weather continued cold and the pulling hard as we moved across Rasmussen Basin toward the Murchison River, which would take us over the Boothia Peninsula. I was anxious to get out of this terrain and onto something I hoped would be easier for the dogs. Still, I took time to study my maps and the landmarks carefully. With dozens of dead-end rivers all around us, it was critical to enter the mountains at the right place. As cold and dark as it was, I couldn't afford to make any mistakes.

DECEMBER 17, 1993   -14°F   BREEZE N   9 MILES

What a mess! The wind blew all night, covering everything with a fine powder. Ice fog, couldn't see much. According to my navigator, we were about a mile from the entrance to the Murchison River. We took off and soon dropped into a riverbed. I stopped and dug down through the snow to make certain we were in a riverbed and not just a narrow valley. Good, flat ice, so off we went south/southeast, with the mountains on my left.

Came to what I thought was a wide place in the river and turned left, east. Then we took a break. Around noon we came to another wide place in the river. Again we turned left. The right looked like a dead end, the bend here seemed to match the map, and Douggie wanted to go left.

At 1:00 P.M., when the dogs stopped to ask for lunch, I knew something was wrong. The mountains were now on my right, but that couldn't be. I turned on the navigator. We were only one mile from where we'd camped last night! Somewhere I'd made a mistake.

I studied the map and found no explanation. The only thing to do was what you always do when you get lost: follow your trail back to where you *know* you know where you are. And start again.

We turned around and started back. When I got to where we'd made our second left turn, I saw my error. The right-hand turn was not a dead end; it was a curve in the river. Coming at it from this angle, I could just barely see the bend behind a small bluff beside the river.

Over half a day wasted. I was furious with myself for wasting so much of the dogs' effort. Altogether we'd traveled nine miles for nothing.

We turned up the Murchison River and began climbing into the mountains, until darkness forced us to stop and make camp. When I tried to heat water for the dogs, I discovered a dangerous problem.

Close Call with Hypothermia

DECEMBER 18, 1993   -45°F   25 M.P.H. W   17 MILES
Stove is dead and I'm too cold to write. The fuel I bought in Gjoa Haven is contaminated. Neither generator will send gas into burner. We are near the top of the pass. The wind is screaming through here.

By the next morning, the wind had picked up even more. Inside the tent, it was almost as cold as outside. Without a working stove, I had no way to warm up. Even inside my sleeping bag, I was so cold that my feet and hands hurt. I didn't want to leave my sleeping bag because getting up would make them hurt more.

Part of me understood that not wanting to move was a classic symptom of hypothermia. Yet I couldn't talk myself into moving. I felt scared, but in a dreamy, disconnected way. My body didn't seem to possess enough energy to care about anything except resting. It would have been so easy to simply lie there and slowly freeze to death, a hundred times easier than getting up. My thoughts moved lazily back and forth, like a fight in very slow motion: *move; don't move; move.*

I'm not sure how long I lay there, trying to motivate myself into action, but eventually I focused on a pile of used wooden matches in the bottom of my broken stove. Without thinking, I slowly reached out, picked up the matches with my stiff fingers, and piled them on the burner. Clumsily, I lit the matches. As soon as they caught, I stuck my head over the miniature fire and inhaled one deep breath of warm air.

Instantly I felt life flowing into my body. It was a sudden burst of energy that seemed unbelievable, like magic, though I suspect it was some sort of chemical reaction in my brain. Whatever the cause, I didn't dare waste it. I jumped up and began getting ready to leave. It took almost no time to get the tent and sled bag packed.

When it came time to harness the dogs, however, I couldn't get them moving. They were overcome by the same cold-induced lethargy I'd struggled with. I pulled each dog up to put its harness on, but by the time I'd finished, they were all curled up on the ground again!

Again I pulled them up, one by one. And again, as soon as I let go, each would lie back down. Finally, I jerked them all up and began screaming at them, "Move! Now! Or we're going to freeze to death!"

They looked thoroughly bedraggled and pathetic. I knew how they felt. We got off to a very unenthusiastic, but essential, start.

DECEMBER 19, 1993   -30°F   30 M.P.H. W   22 MILES

Soon the dogs realized that the pulling was easier as we moved across the flat top of the pass. The big uphill pull was finished. Then they started to run, and I think they actually had fun. Because I couldn't melt snow, they had to eat dry food for lunch and were snatching mouthfuls of snow to ease their thirst. I can't help that right now.

The stove, including both tank/generator assemblies, is indeed dead. The contamination in the fuel is debris that looks like brown paper, maybe some sort of seal from the fuel drum.

I can't make any water. The dogs got some dry food and caribou and sausage from my rations. I hope the fat will help them with dehydration. I ate my food raw. Nothing like eating rice and margarine raw. Actually, they tasted pretty good. The steak is so hard I can't bite into it without worrying about breaking my teeth. The cheese is like cardboard, but at least it's edible. Thank heavens for logan bread. Lots of fat and calories in it, and it never freezes so hard that I can't eat it.

Once I thought I saw a light up ahead while we were traveling in the dark, but now I think it was only a star. My glasses are useless in this cold, even my frost-resistant ones. It makes navigating a real challenge, but I'm sort of used to it now.

As we continued along the riverbed, traveling downhill, only a few patches of hard snow remained. The dogs slipped continually on the glare ice. Even worse, there was almost no snow for them to lick. They were thirsty all the time and becoming famished. With no other choice, we continued our diet of frozen food and whatever snow we could find to melt in our mouths.

It was tough going, but the only alternative was freezing and starving to death. I tried to focus on a few small, but positive, facts. The wind had died down a little. Since we were moving southeast, we had a little more light to cover more miles. And we were getting close to the next town, Pelly Bay, a Native community of about 220 people where more supplies would be waiting.

DECEMBER 21, 1993   -40°F   10 M.P.H.   W   35 MILES

Another nightmare start. It was blizzarding, and now my headlamp is trying to give me trouble. It keeps blinking on and off, mostly off, and makes working around camp a pain. The wind died down around late morning.

I hope we're on the right river. It's hard to tell even with the map and navigator. There are lots of sandbars and gravel beds among the glare-ice fields. Pulling is very hard for the dogs. We keep wandering around, trying to avoid all these things. So it slows our progress.

Once we came across a caribou skull with nothing on it, but the dogs attacked it and tried to eat it anyway. They are getting really hungry. All I can do is give them dry food. We're getting low on everything except fuel. Lots of contaminated fuel.

The river we're on, a segment of the Murchison, goes to the bay called Pelly Bay. The town of Pelly Bay is on the other side, maybe twenty miles across. I don't want to try crossing in anything but daylight because I've heard that it's a very bad place. The ice is all rubble.

Nightmare Ice

DECEMBER 22, 1993   -38°F   5 M.P.H.   W   25 MILES

We started out over Pelly Bay, had good going for two miles, and then hit incredibly rough ice. Douggie took commands and worked well for a while, but he got stressed out. Anna had to take over. It seemed as though we'd never get through this nightmare ice. The rubble was only about two or three feet high, but it was packed solid. No way but to axe my way through.

Then we had incredible luck. I came across a frozen lead that took us for about a mile; then a little ridge of ice, then more frozen lead; then rubble, then more lead. The lead took us too far to the southeast and zigzagged a lot, but it certainly was better than hacking through all that bad stuff. It took us three-fourths of the way across the bay.

When we ran out of lead it started to get dark. I wasn't going to spend another night in the cold. We had almost nothing left to eat, and I was tired of being so cold.

I knew we were too far south, so I began hacking toward the northeast in the dark. Finally I came across some fairly fresh snowmachine tracks and followed them. The tracks took us to shore and onto a trail that headed north. Suddenly the lights of Pelly Bay were ahead. The dogs saw them, too, and began running. Food and rest were in sight!

But the lights seemed to take forever to get any closer. Then, just as suddenly as they had appeared, they disappeared. Douggie looked around, trying to figure out what had happened. I searched, too. The lights were nowhere to be seen.

We continued in the same direction, hoping to find the lights again. After quite a while, they reappeared.

Then we hit more rubble. I was so worn out that I felt like crying. The dogs were as confused as I was.

I stepped off the sled and tramped through the rubble, making a sort of trail for the dogs to follow. Then I rode the sled through, stopped, and repeated the process, over and over. The sled kept getting stuck, I kept falling down, and we kept meeting more rubble.

Once I stopped and swore at the top of my lungs in sheer frustration. It didn't do much good, but I felt a little better.

Then, once again, the lights disappeared.

Finally I figured out that many small islands just offshore were blocking our view. We'd been shifting back and forth in the dark between sea ice and land, seeking a passable route. I pulled the team in to shore at a point I hoped was close to the town. Just then an elderly Inuk man walked by! He spoke no English, and I couldn't speak enough Inuktituk to say anything useful, so we just laughed at ourselves. The man waved good-bye and walked on.

A few minutes later, as I was unharnessing the dogs, a young man on a snowmobile arrived. He turned out to be the son of the elderly fellow and gave me a ride into Pelly Bay. As quickly as possible, I found my supplies at the school, soaked some dry dog food, and returned to the team. They were curled up behind piles of ice, sleeping. In a few more minutes they were happily fed, watered, and resting out of the wind.

Soon I, too, was safe and warm and well fed at the home of Maurice, Patsy, and Tara Randall, who had invited me to stay with them. As my body revived, so did my spirits. A huge sense of relief and happiness filled me. We'd made it through another rough segment of the trip. And there was only one more leg to go!

At last I was certain we would finish. After all we'd been through, nothing could stop us now.

Pelly Bay Christmas

▼ *Christmas in Pelly Bay. The entire community of 220 people met in the school gymnasium on Christmas Eve to watch Santa give presents to every child.*

By the time we'd rested up, it was Christmas. I decided to celebrate the holiday in Pelly Bay.

On Christmas Day everyone in town gathered at the community center, which doubles as a gymnasium and auditorium. People were seated all around the edges of the room. Santa came in and gave every kid in town a gift, calling each one by name. Though I'd appeared in the village as a stranger just a few days before, even I received a present—eight large fish for the dogs! I was very grateful.

A ten-day community celebration was under way. Inside the community center, traditional Eskimo-Indian Olympic games took place around the clock. Outside there were dog races, which I watched but didn't participate in because I wanted my dogs to rest. Services were held at the Anglican and Roman Catholic churches. There seemed to be a constant supply of food and laughter shared all around.

It was a wonderful, festive holiday. Except for one nagging detail, I might have stayed for the entire ten days. We still had an expedition to finish.

Once again, I packed up the sled and said good-bye to warmth, companionship, and comfort, to hit the cold, dark trail. But this time I was too excited to even think about missing civilization. The end of our expedition was practically within sight. Only 228 miles out of 2,500 remained.

Can't Stop Us Now!

DECEMBER 28, 1993   -38°F   12 M.P.H. SW   16 MILES

Got up and fixed breakfast of two eggs and loaded everything on sleds. About twelve miles out, caribou appeared in the dusky ice fog. I had my hands out of my gloves, with my fingers curled up, trying to get them warm, when the dogs started after the caribou. I got jerked off my feet, but hung on to the tether line to the trailer sled for a few seconds. Then I lost my grip.

Was this any way to finish an expedition? Before I knew it, I was being dragged across the tundra by my right foot, which was caught in the yoke of the trailer sled. Fortunately, I was dragged only about a hundred feet. Not so fortunately, my boot continued without me. As the dogs disappeared into the mist, I was left stranded at -38°F with only my left boot.

But luck was with me that day, after all. Within a few minutes of walking, I found my right boot. For the time being, then, I didn't have to worry about my foot freezing. I walked for about an hour, following the dogs' trail, until I found them in some deep snow, waiting ever so patiently and sweetly.

The truth was, they couldn't do much else. The sled was stuck fast against a large rock. Without me to free it, my four-legged delinquents weren't going anywhere.

I, of course, insisted we forget the caribou and sled back to our trail. By then it was too late to continue, so we made camp. I was very tired, but even more relieved that no one had been hurt. All we'd lost was time.

We headed toward the Kellett River, which would take us across the Simpson Peninsula to Committee Bay.

DECEMBER 29, 1993   -35°F   2 M.P.H. W   22 MILES

Dropped down onto the Kellett River. The river turns a lot and has steep, rocky walls, gorge-like in many places. The snow is dirty and sandy. Saw more caribou and had the usual confusion—but I didn't lose the team this time.

A good day today, but very cold. Mostly, keeping my hands warm is the biggest problem. My feet even got a little cold today, but not painful. I think because the insulating socks inside the boots are worn out and have big holes, my feet have trouble keeping warm. In the beginning, last year, my feet stayed warm all the time.

DECEMBER 30, 1993   -54°F   8 M.P.H   SW   11 MILES

Not a good day. Woke up forty-five minutes late! Moved slowly, even though I thought I was moving fast. The low temperature changes your perspective on speed.

It's easy to get lost in these rolling hills. Uphill in this cold is very hard on all of us. Everything creaks at this temperature. Even when I turn my head, my parka hood creaks! Everything seems to be in slow motion. The dogs seem okay with the temperature. The problem is the increased friction against the sled runners as the snow crystals contract in the severe cold.

A very clear sky, and deep pink in the evening. I think I'll see the sun soon.

DECEMBER 31, 1993   -56°F   15 M.P.H.   SW   18 MILES

Tomorrow starts a new year, but soon brings to a close a long trip. Tonight the moon is full. The northern lights stream across the southern horizon under a clear but ice-foggy sky. It's so quiet and peaceful and beautiful here, alone with my dogs. I love them all. Tonight, as I finished feeding and petting them and saying my good-nights, I thought I am the luckiest person alive on this Earth right now. I have food, shelter, warmth, my dogs, and solitude. I have all I need.

We reached Committee Bay on the first day of the new year. The ice on the bay was the worst I'd seen on this trip, so I tried to stay on the beach as much as possible. Looking across the bay, the ice appeared impenetrable.

Temperatures continued cold, sapping our energy and causing extra drag against the sled runners. The country seemed to be a maze of rolling hills folded into one another like lumpy blankets. It was easy to get lost and hard to stay on track. The terrain and bad ice forced us to twist and turn relentlessly.

JANUARY 2, 1994   -30°F   25 M.P.H.   NW   24 MILES

How can it be that we seemed to go so fast and traveled only twenty-four miles? Maybe there are more twists and turns on our route than I realize. We sled on slick, shore-fast ice until bad ice up ahead is visible. Then we go up on the beach, which usually slopes toward the ice quite a bit. We sled on the very, very edge of the land, where there appears to be a sort of alley between the land and rough ice of the bay.

The wind was very high all day, but thankfully, mostly at our backs. The dogs hate the wind. When we stop, they curl up quickly. I try to take short breaks in areas protected by cliffs. The wind is noisy and the snow blows constantly. The sky is clear overhead, but clouds are all around the horizon. Gray, mostly. No sun. I thought it might appear today.

We must do better tomorrow. Otherwise, I'll have to start rationing food. Lucy, Matt, and Alice are a little fat, so I'm cutting their rations today, anyway.

The next day, as we crested a ridge and began heading down toward the beach, we started moving downhill way too fast. I stood on the brake with all my weight, calling, "Easy! Easy!" But the sleds were in danger of running over the dogs or careening completely out of control. So I stopped and turned loose Anna, Robert, Sojo, and Alice. As they ran ahead, the rest of us followed more slowly behind.

Suddenly, I saw the loose dogs down on the beach. Oddly, they looked very small. I realized there must be a big drop-off between us.

Sure enough, when I parked the team and walked ahead, I discovered what was probably a waterfall in summer! There was no way we could sled down it. So I set the other four dogs loose to find their way down to the beach. Then I pushed each sled carefully to the edge and over. They dropped about fifteen feet straight down. I followed the dogs down a snow chute, sliding on the seat of my pants.

Dogs, driver, and sleds all reached bottom safely. I hooked everyone up again and off we went, feeling cheerier for the unexpected diversion.

That night we camped on the open tundra, on snow so wind-packed my shovel didn't make a dent in the stuff. I had to chop snow with a hatchet to melt it for water.

JANUARY 4, 1994   -30°F   2 M.P.H.   W   11 MILES

Great start—got past Point Hargrave and went behind an island. Then, as we tried to round a point, the rubble ice came up to shore.

I've made a big mistake. I should have turned inland by a creek a long ways back. Now we're camped in rubble. It looks pretty bleak; bad ice as far as I can see.

At least an end is in sight. This part of the trip is much harder than I expected, due to this terrible ice. The dogs are bummed—but it's very good command training, weaving through the rubble ice.

Dogs do best if they're allowed to make some decisions on their own. If they have to take commands every few seconds, as they do in rubble ice, it wears them out mentally and they feel stressed. The dogs' heads are low to the ground, so from their perspective the rubble must look impenetrable. Even the best, strongest-minded leaders have trouble in this type of situation. Anna and Douggie sometimes stopped and simply stared ahead, totally confused. Often during this stretch, I had to walk ahead, make a trail with my footsteps, then walk back to the sled and proceed together until my trail ran out. I repeated the process over and over. It was very slow going.

There was one bright spot, literally. On January 4 I saw the sun for the first time in thirty days. At first it peeked through a notch in the hills; then, as we rounded a corner, I saw it fully. It was mostly orange, with a touch of yellow. The light wasn't very intense—I could look straight at it without having a blind spot when I looked away—but somehow it still felt warm. And reassuring. Even though I knew the sun would come back, after several sunless weeks I couldn't help feeling relieved to see it sitting up there in the sky.

We left the rubble-strewn shores of Committee Bay and headed overland, up a river valley through mountainous terrain, toward Repulse Bay. The tundra we crossed was dotted with frozen lakes.

JANUARY 6, 1994   -22°F   15 M.P.H.   NW   12 MILES

Only had one-quarter mile of rubble ice and then it flattened out as we passed a river exit. Still had large icebergs to go around, but lots of room to maneuver. Thank God we are out of that mess! Another day in that rubble and my brain would've been rubble.

The wind is making the water shift beneath the ice, and the ice is booming all over this no-name lake. The water we're on must be fresh water; the ice is smooth and very hard. The bare ice looks black. As we sled over it I can see down into it. Always it's honeycombed with cracks that look like white knife slashes.

On the ocean, the ice is almost always uneven. The surface is covered with billions of small cauliflower-like bumps—white, crusty, and about an inch in diameter.

It's better traveling on freshwater ice because it's flatter and easier on the dogs' feet. Also it's easier to get good snow for melting into water. As the temperature drops tonight, the ice expands. Sometimes it groans and then sounds like it explodes, like a string of firecrackers going off.

I knew from my maps that we were getting very close to Repulse Bay — less than fifty miles!

JANUARY 8, 1994   -40°F   5 M.P.H.   SW   26 MILES

We got off to a good start, and early, too. Soon the dogs slowed down, though. I think because we've traveled through some rough country and they haven't had a day off in twelve days. Too bad I made that mistake in Committee Bay, or we'd be in Repulse Bay by now. Oh, well.

We crossed Wilson Lake and came out on the end of a little creek. The dogs and I all heard the sound of a snowmobile. Suddenly I saw two coming. Two men from Repulse Bay! The younger man spoke English, the older man Inuktituk. They were going ice fishing. We talked briefly and I told them where I was from. They seemed surprised.

We followed their trail — really nice for the dogs. Then we had to climb for a couple miles over a long, long rise; then a lake; then a three-mile climb. The climbing and friction and cold really took it out of the dogs. I knew as we started out of the pass that even though the rest was mostly downhill, we wouldn't reach Repulse Bay in the daylight.

I guess one more night out on the trail will be okay. I sort of like it. Our last night on the trail together.

Tomorrow, an easy twenty miles to Repulse Bay.

Those last twenty miles were indeed downhill. But as it turned out — I should have known better by then! — they were not particularly easy. We ended up sledding down a riverbed on glare ice that was studded everywhere with boulders, rocks, and gravel. It was a good thing this was our last day, because the rocks and gravel ruined what was left of my sled runners.

Finally we came out onto perfectly flat ice on Repulse Bay. I could see the town in the distance, about three miles away. The dogs couldn't have seen it, but they must have smelled it. With no command from me, they suddenly broke into a trot, and then an all-out run, racing as fast as they could.

I started jumping up and down on the sled, yelling and hooting at the top of my lungs. All the while, the dogs kept running their fastest. When I almost fell off the sled, I decided I'd better calm down. Otherwise, the dogs would arrive in Repulse Bay without a driver!

That last mile, I just watched the dogs. They looked so fit, so free, moving so swiftly and with such ease. I let the beauty and joy of it soak into me. Very best of all, every dog was still with me. None had failed; none had been lost. All nine of us had made it, together.

Then the Arctic handed me one more totally frustrating, last-minute challenge. The final hundred yards to shore were nothing but rubble ice!

The sled slammed into a ledge of ice and we were stuck. I couldn't believe it. Rather than sledding gloriously into Repulse Bay, as I'd imagined, we were going to have to grunt, groan, and heave our way forward, just as we'd done for so many other miles.

There was no way around it. I pushed and pulled the sled free. We moved forward a few feet and got stuck again. I pushed and pulled some more. Over and over again, that's how we proceeded.

As I was busy busting a path through the rubble, a group of people walked toward us. One of them was the mayor of Repulse Bay. He introduced himself, congratulated us, and took our picture. Then everyone helped us negotiate those final few yards to shore.

JANUARY 9, 1994   -40°F   8 M.P.H.   N   20 MILES
Arrived Repulse Bay about 1:30 P.M. Mayor and about ten others came down to greet me. Happy to be here!

On shore everyone shook my hand. After so much time alone, the eleven men seemed like a giant crowd. On the outside I was smiling and saying "thank you" to everyone; inside, I felt overcome by so many emotions it was impossible to sort them out in the confusion and excitement of the moment.

Memories of the previous fifteen months tumbled through my mind. In the beginning, I'd felt the excitement of the challenge. During the journey, I'd experienced the exhaustion of long days on a cold trail, the frustration of plans gone wrong, the fear of failure, as well as the joy and confidence that comes from winning many small victories. Now I felt the pride of having finally succeeded in reaching our goal.

After the men had gone and I stood there alone with my team, one word came to mind that summarized all of my emotions together: respect. I felt tremendous respect for every one of my dogs, and respect for myself.

The dogs, I believe, felt it too. We'd done well, and in doing so, had won what I consider the greatest reward of all: self-respect. We carry it with us wherever we go. ☾

Epilogue

I spent the next few days in Repulse Bay, resting and making arrangements to get home. A newspaper reporter named Judy Langford had taken an interest in the expedition and convinced Calm Air to transport me, as well as my dogs, sleds, and gear, to Churchill, Manitoba. From there we rode the train, courtesy of VIA Rail, to Winnipeg.

In Winnipeg I was given free use of a U-Haul moving truck to drive home to Alaska. I paid for the gas with my heavily burdened credit card. The trip was entirely uneventful, except for one problem. For more than twelve months I hadn't traveled faster than about fifteen miles per hour. Now, driving the truck, I couldn't push the speedometer beyond forty miles per hour! Any higher speed was terrifying. (Almost a year passed before I could drive comfortably at fifty-five m.p.h.)

I reached home tired and deeply in debt. But I felt immensely satisfied. I'd fulfilled my dream, experiencing an adventure most people could scarcely imagine. Best of all, I did it without hurting or losing any of my dogs.

Would I do it again? Yes!

And maybe I will.

▲ *Since completing this journey, I have returned to the Far North many times, always certain there is enough magic in the Arctic to make my dreams come true.*

Expedition Supply List

Following is a complete list of the items I used during the expedition. Some items — such as batteries, gloves, socks, dog food, tea, rice, flour, film, maps, and paper products — were mailed ahead to the communities I visited along my route. Others could not be shipped but were purchased along the way (these included fuel, meat, cheese, vegetables, and occasional cans of fruit).

Dogsleds (2)
Sled bag
Snowhooks (3)
Tarp
Dog food
  (2,000 pounds)
Dog food cook pot
Stir stick
Dog bowls
Harnesses (10)
Extra brass snaps (3)
Extra sections 1/2"
  line (3)
Extra sections 3/8"
  line (6)
50' 1/8" line
Dog nail clippers
Dog booties
Dog foot ointment
Toy sled (used to
  ferry goods over
  pressure ridges and
  around towns)
Expedition parka
Expedition pants
Expedition hat
Expedition boots
Expedition boot liner
Expedition mitts
Neoprene face masks
  (3)
Polypro underwear
  (2 tops)
Polypro underwear
  (2 bottoms)
Wool socks (6 pairs
  small)
Wool socks (6 pairs
  medium)
Polypro gloves
  (4 pairs small)
Polypro gloves
  (4 pairs medium)

Wool gloves (2 pairs
  small)
Wool gloves (2 pairs
  medium)
Sweater
T-shirt
Underpants (7)
Emergency plastic
  bag of dry clothing
  (top and bottom
  Polypro underwear,
  gloves, pants,
  sweater, socks)
Ice probe
Topographic maps
  (44)
Magnetic compasses
  (2)
Small, handheld
  calculator
Map wheel
Navigator (GPS)
Navigator case
AA batteries (60)
Anemometer
Trail markers
Thermometer
Thermometer case
Sextant
Artificial horizon
ELT (emergency
  locator transmitter)
ELT case
Emergency flares (6)
First aid items
  (aspirin, bandages,
  antibiotics [human
  and canine],
  antibiotic cream,
  decongestant, throat
  lozenges, antacid
  tablets)
Shotgun
Shotgun case

Ammunition (slugs
  and 00 buck)
Graphite lubricant
Shovel
Keyhole saw
Hatchet
Carabiners
Tent
Tent stakes
Sleeping bag
Sleeping mats
Sleeping jacket
Sleeping pants
Sleeping hat
Sleeping boots
Spare eyeglasses
Hard glasses case
Diary
Pencil
Personal items
  (hairbrush, tooth-
  brush, toothpaste,
  deodorant, soap)
People food (steak,
  rice, frozen
  vegetables, sausage,
  cheese, logan bread,
  dried fruits,
  nuts, tea, hot
  chocolate mix)
Vitamins
Stove
Stove board
Stove tank/generator
  (spare)
Stove repair kit
Matches (4 boxes)
Fire ribbon
Fuel
Fuel funnel (2)
Coffee pot
Covered pot
Fry pan
Bowl

Fork
Knife
Pliers
Screwdriver
Nail clippers
Repair kit (sewing
  needles; dental floss
  for thread; duct
  tape; approximately
  18" harness
  material, 12" Velcro,
  and 10' yarn)
Paperback book
  (traded in each
  community)
Headlamp
Headlamp batteries,
  D cell (48)
Headlamp spare
  bulbs (2)
Headlamp wire
Paper towels (3 rolls)
Toilet paper (6 rolls)
Plastic gallon freezer
  bags (2)
Plastic quart freezer
  bags (6)
Thermos
Thermos bag
Stuff sacks
Video camera
Fur cover for video
  camera
Video camera
  batteries (2)
Video film
35mm camera
35mm camera case
35mm film (60 rolls)
Camera batteries (2)
Tripod
Monopod

Glossary

ANEMOMETER: An instrument used to measure the speed, or force, of the wind.

ARCTIC CHAR: A species of fish found in northern salt waters.

ARCTIC NATIONAL WILDLIFE REFUGE: One of the largest U.S. wildlife refuges, located on Alaska's North Slope. Controversy continues over whether to allow development in this refuge.

BOOTIES: Fleece socks for the dogs. Held in place by Velcro, they protect the dogs' footpads from becoming chafed or cut. Booties are used most often in conditions of rough ice or grainy snow.

BREAKUP: The time of year when the snow and ice start melting. The ice on rivers and lakes "breaks up" into pieces.

CACHE: A place where provisions are stored for later use.

COMMANDS: The words used by mushers to tell their lead dogs what to do. Some common commands are: *gee* (go right); *haw* (go left); *hike* (go); and *whoa* (stop). I (and many other mushers) say *all right* instead of *hike*.

COMPASS HEADING: A course of direction determined by using a compass.

"CROW" MILES: My term for the shortest distance between two points, "as the crow flies." Most often the number of actual miles traveled is greater.

DEW LINE (distant early warning line): A series of radar stations built across northern Alaska and Canada in the 1950s as part of a military defense system. Many have been abandoned because new technology has made them obsolete.

ELT (emergency locator transmitter): An instrument that, when activated, emits a signal that is relayed via satellite systems to various emergency response locations around the world to initiate search and rescue.

ESKIMO DOG: A northern breed of dog with an extremely dense coat, short snout, and round head.

ESKIMO-INDIAN OLYMPICS: Games and competitions traditional to the indigenous peoples of Alaska and Canada that are held annually in various communities in northern North America. The World Eskimo-Indian Olympics draw Native American athletes together to compete in games such as the knuckle hop, one-foot and two-foot high kick, stick pull, and ear-weight competition.

GANGLINE: A system of ropes running from the front of a dogsled. The dogs are attached to the gangline by short lines that clip onto the dogs' harnesses. Dogs usually run in pairs, one dog on each side of the gangline.

GLARE ICE: Hard, slick ice.

GPS (global positioning system): A handheld device that receives information from satellites to display the latitude and longitude of its location. I also refer to it as a "navigator."

HAUL OUT: The action of seals and walruses as they pull themselves out of the sea onto ice or land.

HYPOTHERMIA: A condition in which the body becomes too cold to maintain its normal temperature and shuts down the flow of blood to hands and feet, then arms and legs, in an attempt to keep warmth in the vital organs. As body temperature drops, a person loses coordination and the ability to think clearly. If not treated, hypothermia eventually results in freezing to death.

ICE FOG: A fog made up of ice crystals.

ICE PROBE: A metal bar with a sharpened point that is thrust into ice to measure its thickness and thus judge its safety for crossing.

IDITAROD TRAIL SLED DOG RACE: A dog-mushing race of approximately 1,200 miles from Anchorage to Nome, Alaska.

INUIT: A name for the indigenous peoples of arctic Alaska, Canada, and Greenland; also still known in Alaska as "Eskimos." *Inuit* means "the people."

INUK: The singular form of *Inuit*; an indigenous person of northern Canada.

INUKSUK: Rocks piled, often in the shape of a person, to mark directions.

INUKTITUK: The language of Canada's Inuit people.

INUPIAT: A name for the indigenous Inuit or Eskimo people of northern Alaska. *Inupiat* also means "the people."

LEAD: An opening of water in sea, river, or lake ice.

MAGNETIC NORTH POLE: The location in the Northern Hemisphere where the Earth's magnetic forces enter the Earth. The Magnetic North Pole shifts continuously.

MOUNT McKINLEY: The tallest mountain in North America. Many Alaskans prefer the name *Denali*, an earlier name derived from a Tanaina Indian word meaning "the Great One" or "the Big One."

MUSH: To travel over snow and ice with a sled pulled by dogs.

MUSK OX: A very large, long-haired mammal that lives in extreme northern regions. Adult females weigh 250 to 500 pounds; adult males weigh up to 900 pounds. By about 1865 all Alaskan musk oxen had been killed by hunters. Since 1932, when thirty-four musk oxen from Greenland were brought to Alaska, the shaggy animals have thrived.

NAVIGATOR: See "GPS."

NORTHERN LIGHTS: A display of lights, often colored, seen in the night skies of the Northern Hemisphere, especially above the Arctic Circle, and caused by electrically charged particles from the sun streaming into Earth's magnetic field. Also called "aurora borealis."

NORTH SLOPE: The region of Alaska that lies north of the Brooks Range and south of the Arctic Ocean.

PEDAL: To stand on a sled runner with one leg while pushing off against the ground repeatedly with the other leg to help move the sled forward.

PINGO: A small rise or mound in an otherwise flat landscape.

PRESSURE RIDGE: A ridge of ice, commonly ranging in height from a few inches up to twenty feet, formed by the pressure of expanding and shifting ice.

PRUDHOE BAY: The center of Alaska's oil industry on the North Slope; refers to both the bay on the Arctic Ocean and the general area surrounding it.

PTARMIGAN: A species of northern grouse with feathered legs and feet.

PUNCHY SNOW: Thinly crusted snow on top of softer snow. Punchy snow is difficult to walk on because footsteps break through the crust.

RUBBLE ICE: Big chunks of broken-up ice on frozen seas or rivers.

SEA ICE: Ice that forms when ocean salt water freezes.

SLED BAG: A heavy cloth bag that is placed in the sled basket and cinched tightly to contain gear and keep out snow.

SLED BASKET: The main body of the sled, where cargo is carried.

SLED BRAKE: A three-pronged metal claw, attached to the floor of the sled, used to stop or slow the sled when it is pressed down with one foot. A spring holds the brake up when not in use.

SNOWHOOK: A heavy, two-pronged, iron hook, attached to the sled with a rope, that is used to anchor the sled by jamming the prongs into the snow. I use two snowhooks to secure the rear of my sled and, sometimes, one to hold the front of the team.

SUBSISTENCE LIVING: The harvest and use of wild and renewable resources, such as fish and game, for personal and family consumption for purposes such as food, shelter, clothing, and other traditional uses.

TUNDRA: Treeless plains of the arctic regions, with low-growing vegetation on top of cold, often frozen, soils.

WIND CHILL: The combined effect of wind and temperature upon body heat. Wind increases the rate at which body heat is lost from exposed skin and causes the air to feel colder than the actual temperature. For example, at 0°F with a 20-m.p.h. wind, the body feels as cold as if it were -22°F.

WHITEOUT: A condition in which light is reflected almost equally from the sky above and the snow below so that almost no shadows are cast, causing the snow and sky to blend into total whiteness.

Index

Index